Discipline in schools

What can schools and teachers do to promote discipline in the classroom? How do discipline and learning interact?

The Elton Committee was set up in 1989 to consider 'what action can be taken to secure the orderly atmosphere necessary in schools for effective teaching and learning to take place'. In this collection of papers, ten leading figures in the psychology of education reflect on some of the issues raised by the Elton Report and provide a series of psychological models for tackling problems of discipline, disorder and disruption in schools. Areas covered include whole-school approaches to discipline, the connection between learning difficulties and discipline problems, the effectiveness of positive behavioural methods of classroom management, the possible uses of techniques derived from family therapy in classroom discipline situations and the 'good relationship' between teacher and student as an agent of change. Though the perspectives of the contributors are very different, the emphasis throughout is on establishing a way forward for schools that will be valid and workable both in institutional terms and for the individual teacher in the classroom.

Kevin Wheldall is Head of the Special Education Division and Director of the Centre for Research into Special Education and Rehabilitation at Macquarie University, Sydney. He is an authority in the area of classroom behaviour management and has published several books and dozens of articles on this subject.

Discipline in schools
Psychological perspectives on the Elton
Report

Edited by
Kevin Wheldall

London and New York

First published 1992 by Routledge
11 New Fetter Lane, London EC4P 4EE

Simultaneously published in the USA and Canada
by Routledge
a division of Routledge, Chapman and Hall, Inc.
29 West 35th Street, New York, NY 10001

© 1992 Kevin Wheldall

Typeset in Times by LaserScript Limited, Mitcham, Surrey
Printed and bound in Great Britain by
Biddles Ltd, Guildford and King's Lynn

British Library Cataloguing in Publication Data
Discipline in schools: psychological perspectives on the
Elton Report.
1. England. Schools, discipline
I. Wheldall, Kevin *1949–*
371.50942

ISBN 0–415–06245–4

Library of Congress Cataloging-in-Publication Data
Discipline in schools: psychological perspectives on the Elton Report/
edited by Kevin Wheldall.
p. cm.
Contributions derived from papers presented at a conference held
in the School of Education, U. of Birmingham and a symposium
presented to the British Psychological Society in 1989.
Includes bibliographical references and index.
ISBN 0–415–06245–4
1. School discipline – Great Britain – Congresses.
2. Classroom management – Great Britain – Congresses.
3. Motivation in education – Congresses. I . Wheldall, Kevin.
LB3012.4.G7D57   1992
371.5 – dc20
91-15700
CIP

Dedication

This is for Rachael Naomi, in the hope that schools will be more positive by the time she begins school.

Contents

Contributors

Dr Roy Bennett was Vice-Chair of the Committee of Enquiry into Discipline in Schools.

Dr Robert Burden is a Senior Lecturer in the School of Education at the University of Exeter.

Dr Paul Cooper is a Research Fellow in the School of Education at the University of Birmingham.

Professor Ted Glynn is Head of the Department of Education at the University of Otago.

Nigel Hastings is a Senior Lecturer in the Department of Education Studies and Management at the University of Reading.

Dr Frank Merrett is a Lecturer/Research Fellow in the Centre for Child Study in the School of Education at the University of Birmingham.

Josh Schwieso is a Lecturer in the Department of Education Studies and Management at the University of Reading.

Colin J. Smith is a Senior Lecturer in the School of Education at the Univer- sity of Birmingham.

Professor Graham Upton is Head of the School of Education at the University of Birmingham.

Professor Kevin Wheldall is Head of the Special Education Division and Director of the Centre for Research into Special Education and Rehabilitation in the School of Education at Macquarie University, Sydney (formerly Director of the Centre for Child Study in the School of Education at the University of Birmingham).

Preface

When Kenneth Baker, the then Secretary of State for Education, announced that a government committee of enquiry had been set up to investigate discipline in schools, it was not greeted warmly by all sections of the educational establishment. I was not alone in voicing, with my research colleague Frank Merrett, misgivings about the whole enterprise. 'It's classroom violence time again', we wrote in an opinion piece in *Teachers' Weekly* in March 1988, '...time for another round of public breast beating by senior politicians about problems of order and control in our schools'. We went on to complain about the way in which teachers' legitimate concerns about discipline had been consistently ignored by Her Majesty's Inspectorate (HMI) (of schools), Local Education Authorities (LEAs) and teacher trainers alike. Reporting our own previous failures to achieve a dialogue with the Department of Education and Science (DES) about our research on effective classroom behaviour management, we concluded in splenetic vein:

> The last thing we need is yet another committee! What we do need from the DES is action to implement what is already clearly and reliably known about how to deal with problems of classroom order and control. These problems are not insurmountable. Solutions are available. Who was it who said, 'When all is said and done, more is said than done'?

Consequently, we were somewhat surprised, if not a little shamefaced, to be called as expert witnesses to Lord Elton's Committee and to have Committee representatives come to discuss our research findings with us at the Centre for Child Study at the University of Birmingham. Moreover, our views were heard sympathetically and the findings of our local research (on what teachers themselves believed to be the most frequent and most troublesome classroom behaviour problems) prompted the Committee to commission an independent national research replication study. (Our findings were subsequently confirmed.)

Another source of astonishment to critics of the Enquiry was the speed at which it moved, commissioning research, making numerous visits, consulting a number of expert witnesses, sifting the evidence and sorting the facts in the midst of a mind-boggling avalanche of opinions and unsubstantiated assertions from a welter of amateur 'experts' who blamed pupil misbehaviour on anything and everything from video nasties to E numbers (food additives) to the abolition of national service. The final Report (DES, 1989) was published in little more than a year after the Committee first met.

The aim of this short book is to provide a series of reaction to the problems posed by the Elton Report on Discipline in Schools. The contributions derive mainly from papers originally presented to a conference on the Elton Report held in the School of Education at the University of Birmingham, and a symposium subsequently presented to the Annual Conference of the Education Section of the British Psychological Society in 1989.

The book begins with an introduction to the Report by the Vice-Chair of the Elton Committee, Roy Bennett. I feel indeed fortunate in having such a well-qualified educationist, and one who can write with such authority, to present a context for and an overview of the Report. This introduction is followed by seven chapters by distinguished psychologists of education reflecting on 'discipline in schools', both in the sense of offering considered responses to the Elton Report itself and also by providing a series of psychological models or approaches for tackling the problems of discipline, disorder and disruption.

The first contribution by my colleague, Frank Merrett, and myself explores the views of experienced teachers about how they learned to manage classroom misbehaviour with particular reference to their initial training for teaching. The available evidence suggests that teachers generally felt ill-equipped to deal with troublesome classroom behaviour following initial courses of training for teaching which barely touched on the skills necessary for effective classroom management.

Ted Glynn, from the University of Otago in New Zealand, spent 1989 on study leave at the Centre for Child Study, University of Birmingham and, hence, was in the UK when the Report was released. Consequently, he was able to offer an 'outsider's perspective' but informed by a sound knowledge of the educational context in which the Report came into being. Drawing on his research and experience in New Zealand, he offers a whole-school model for approaching discipline policy.

Colin Smith has been active in the overlapping fields of learning and behaviour difficulties for many years. He is too wise and wiley a bird to subscribe to the ill-supported notion favoured by many teacher educators that poor discipline results from inadequate lesson preparation. Instead, he argues in his chapter that a failure to recognise and remediate learning difficulties may frequently result in the creation of behaviour difficulties in pupils who find that school has little or nothing to offer them.

Robert Burden, eclectic in his expertise and interests within the field of educational psychology, advocates (like Glynn) a whole-school approach to discipline and behaviour problems. He describes preliminary work adapting a Western Australian approach for use in British Schools.

The second contribution by Frank Merrett and myself is based on our ten-year research programme (the Positive Teaching Project) on effective classroom behaviour management carried out from the Centre for Child Study at the University of Birmingham, between 1981 and 1990. We summarise the research evidence we presented to the Committee of Enquiry as invited expert witnesses and which is referred to in the Elton Report. This chapter is based on the Eleventh Schonell Memorial Lecture which I presented at the University of Queensland in October 1990.

Paul Cooper and Graham Upton have been active in developing a new method for considering behaviour difficulties, which they term an 'eco-systemic' approach. In their chapter, they show how many of the conceptualisations and techniques derived from family therapy may be applied in schools. An extended version of this chapter has appeared in the journal *Educational Psychology*.

Nigel Hastings offers, in his chapter, a thought-provoking re-analysis of the evidence for behaviour change. Whilst having written and researched from within a behavioural framework, he argues that the models espoused by researchers may not be congruent with those employed by teachers to explain changes in pupil behaviour.

Finally, Josh Schwieso offers a critical commentary on the views, models and approaches offered by these psychologists of varying theoretical persuasions and considers how far they go towards meeting the challenge for reform offered by the Elton Report. Clearly there are no right answers at this stage.

We might argue that many of the decisions to be taken are empirical questions to be solved by data-based decision making, but since when has the world of education been much bothered by data? As the Elton Committee discovered, everybody had theories about discipline and disruption in schools but few concerned themselves with facts or empirical findings. A cynic might claim that this is why we rarely see progress in education but merely changes of fashion. Time will tell. But I cannot help suspecting that, for all the undoubted virtues of the Elton Report, we will see the same debates continuing in the years to come. Problems of discipline and disruptive behaviour will, like the poor, always be with us.

Kevin Wheldall
Sydney

1 *Discipline in Schools*: the Report of the Committee of Enquiry chaired by Lord Elton

Roy Bennett

During the time that Lord Elton's Committee was at work, newspapers regularly referred to our task in terms of violence in schools. This is understandable when one remembers that our committee was established in the aftermath of some very serious violent incidents which had aroused justifiable concern in the teachers' professional associations and among parents. This tendency to focus exclusively on the question of violence led, in some quarters, to false expectations about the kind of report we would produce. It is, therefore, important to emphasise that we were given the much wider task of considering 'what action can be taken...to secure the orderly atmosphere necessary in schools for effective teaching and learning to take place' (DES, 1989, p.54).

In seeking possible answers to that question, between March 1988 and January 1989 we held regular meetings, read a mass of written evidence submitted by organisations and individuals, looked at research evidence already published, interviewed expert witnesses, visited a wide range of schools and other institutions in this country and paid study visits to the USA, Norway and the Netherlands. In arriving at our conclusions in a relatively short period of time we were fortunate in two respects: we had the guidance of very experienced and well-informed assessors from both the DES and HMI and we had the services of an efficient and unstinting secretariat. That we quickly established a consensus which allowed us to produce a unanimous report owed much to the fact that all members of the committee had substantial experience of working with children and young people in schools or elsewhere.

We were frequently asked whether discipline in schools is deteriorating. Our inability to provide an authoritative answer to that question clearly came as a great disappointment to some journalists and some teachers, but there simply does not exist the kind of historical database which would enable comparisons to be drawn with any confidence. Although there is a widespread perception, among teachers and the general public, that indiscipline is increasing, there is no way of telling how that perception may have been affected by inaccurate rose-tinted assumptions about schools in the past, or by widespread publicity, raised expectations and the stress of unremitting institutional change to which teachers have been subjected in recent years. Certainly no historian would be able to identify a period when the behaviour of pupils did not give their teachers cause for anxiety. Teachers have always had to battle against inattention, idleness, irresponsibility, vandalism, bullying, fighting, defiance, truancy, impertinence and personal assault. In one very important sense our inability to decide whether these aspects of pupils' behaviour in schools were deteriorating does not really matter very much. The fact that many people think that things are getting worse is an important consideration in its own right. That belief will colour the way the education service is viewed, and it will affect the way in which incidents are interpreted. It will influence public and political attitudes to individual schools and teachers, it will affect the way in which teachers approach their work and it will tend to erode the morale of the teaching profession.

Naturally, those who believe that indiscipline is on the increase were eager to search our report for evidence which would indict certain groups as being to blame for this state of affairs. Our Report does not seek to apportion blame, partly because the range of influences to which individual pupils are subjected is both extensive and infinitely varied, and partly because the most appropriate people to take action to cope with the problems will not necessarily be those who have helped to create those problems in the first place. Certainly those journalists who assumed that we were placing the blame on teachers, because many of our recommendations are addressed to schools, were jumping to a false conclusion. It should be seen more as an indication of our faith in the teachers' professional expertise and resourcefulness, our admiration of the good practice which already exists in so many schools, and our conviction that, whatever policy initiatives are proposed, it will inevitably be the individual teacher's confidence, skill and good sense which will be tested in every instance of indiscipline.

It is, of course, the violent manifestations of indiscipline which hit the headlines and our committee deplored, as much as anyone, the fact that behaviour of this kind occurs in school from time to time. Even one case of violence is one too many. We were, however, impressed by the weight of research evidence indicating that most teachers were more 'concerned about the cumulative effects of disruption to their lessons caused by relatively trivial but persistent misbehaviour' (DES, 1989, p.11) (see Chapter 6). The survey of teachers' opinions which we commissioned from Sheffield University confirmed us in that view. Deliberate violence directed at teachers is relatively rare considering the total numbers of teachers and pupils in our schools: constant disruption, noise, idleness and minor skirmishing appear to be dispiriting, energy-sapping and stressful features of the daily lives of most teachers. It seems reasonable to assume that a significant number of the major violent incidents probably arise from the escalation of minor examples of indiscipline which, at the outset, might well be indistinguishable from dozens of similar exchanges between pupils and teachers in the course of a school day.

One of the most striking features of our evidence is the sheer variety of causes of, and cures for, bad behaviour in schools which was suggested to us....It is clear that most of the individuals and organisations submitting evidence consider that bad behaviour in schools is a complex problem which does not lend itself to simple solutions....Any quest for a single dramatic remedy, such as a major piece of new legislation, would be futile.

(DES, 1989, p.64)

Indeed, to suggest that there could be some magic wand, or some easy answer guaranteed A1 at Lloyds, would be to undervalue the interpersonal skills needed by teachers and to practise a cruel deception on young people seeking to enter our very demanding profession. 'Reducing bad behaviour is a realistic aim. Eliminating it completely is not' (DES, 1989, p.65).

During our visits to schools we occasionally encountered individual teachers, and even entire school staffs, who were suffering from low morale. They were pessimistic because they saw themselves as ill-supported and poorly rewarded professionals condemned to battle against the indiscipline generated by such adverse tides in society as the decline in respect for authority, the rejection of moral standards, the break-up of families, unemployment, selfish materialism and the emphasis on violence for entertainment in the media. Obviously, there is no way in which schools can be insulated against the influences that are at work in society generally and, in some areas, schools face more than a fair share of such problems.

Even in the most deprived areas, however, we also found individual teachers and entire school staffs who spoke with genuine enthusiasm and optimism. They recognised the problems but their morale was high because of good leadership and because they felt that, by determination, resource-fulness and flexibility, they were evolving effective strategies for motivating and controlling their pupils. They also felt confident that they would be adequately supported in times of crisis. Such schools were often achieving far more than one might have anticipated judging by the localities in which they were situated.

From visits to these schools we came to share the optimism of their teachers and we became convinced that individual teachers and individual school staffs can make a considerable difference to the behaviour of pupils and to their educational attainments. This view is also supported by some recent academic research. Where teachers approach their work with this optimistic assumption, morale tends to improve but there is nothing more dispiriting than the feeling that one is being swept along helplessly, like so much flotsam, on uncontrollable tidal currents generated in an uncaring society.

In writing our Report we tried to make recommendations which would help to create conditions in which fewer teachers would take a pessimistic view of their daily work and more would find grounds for optimism. We have tried to be positive and there is little that is particularly striking or novel. Indeed, our Report has sometimes been described as 'just common-sense', which I regard as high praise!

Many of our recommendations are based on the good practice which we came to admire in those schools which had created an orderly and caring ethos. We believe that those conditions could and should be more widely established in our schools.

I do not propose to attempt to present here a summary of our Report. All schools have, I understand, received copies and I hope you will find time to read it. But perhaps I could direct your attention to certain key features of the Report.

The quality of the individual teacher is so important that we have quite a lot to say about how they should be selected. How can we help young people decide their own suitability for teaching? How should training institutions select students? How should schools select new teachers, supply teachers, ancillary staff, senior teachers, headteachers? How should staff be allocated to the different roles within a school? In the rare cases where this arises, how should staff be selected for dismissal?

On this question of selection I have two comments to make. The first is in response to those people who suggest that we should only permit students to qualify if they can be guaranteed as capable of teaching effectively in the most difficult schools. You simply could not find 400,000 people of that kind and the education system contains such a variety of schools that we have to accept that people may be perfectly effective as teachers in some parts of the system, even though they might founder in other parts. This emphasises, of course, the selection process in individual schools where it ought to be easier to assess the likelihood of applicants being able to teach effectively in the precise conditions that are to be found there, and which are well known to those making the appointment.

My second comment on selection is that, as the Report points out to the Secretary of State, 'able young people are unlikely to leave school wanting to be teachers if they see the job as having low status and being unrewarding' (DES, 1989, p.86). Morale, pay and conditions of service all affect recruitment to the profession, and the whole idea of carefully selecting the most suitable staff will be unrealistic if there are insufficient applicants to provide a choice. In some places and in some shortage subjects, that problems already exists.

Another topic to which we frequently turn in our Report is staff training. There is a school of thought which believes that maintaining discipline in the classroom depends primarily on the personal charisma of the teacher and on the teacher's astuteness in learning from the trials and errors of hard-won experience. There is, of course, more than a grain of truth in that view. It would be splendid if the education service could be staffed entirely by natural teachers with the charisma to charm birds off the trees but I do not think that such people can be found in sufficient numbers, especially when those qualities can earn much higher salaries in other types of employment. It is important, therefore, that the sincere commitment and conscientious application of teachers at all levels should be supported by appropriate training in group management skills and interpersonal relationships. Our committee was convinced that training could make a significant contribution to reducing the incidence of indiscipline in schools.

We examined or observed a number of different training approaches which appeared to meet the needs of students and teachers who had taken part in them. Training which tackles the problem of discipline directly and explicitly is needed in initial teacher training. It is unreasonable to expect students to infer effective classroom practice from the general principles which they encounter in such course elements as philosophy, psychology or sociology. There also seems to be a need for further training of this type in the induction of newly qualified teachers, in the professional development of teachers at various levels, for the difficult role of supply teachers, with the new category of licensed teachers and in equipping headteachers and senior staff for their supportive role in relation to the discipline problems of other teachers. Training of school governors and school ancillary staff (especially dinner supervisors) is also, in our view, essential.

I hope that the teaching profession will not feel that devising a variety of training approaches and learning resources for these various categories is a task which should be left to outside experts. The profession includes a large number of very experienced, imaginative and outstandingly successful practitioners who should be encouraged to explore ways in which they could share their skills and insights with a wider audience.

We must not, however, delude ourselves into thinking that training will always provide some ready to hand, instant, guaranteed solution to every discipline problem which can be encountered in schools. All that training can do is to indicate some possible pitfalls and widen the repertoire of options from which a teacher can select a course of action when trying to prevent a problem arising or getting worse. In making their decisions teachers will still have to exercise their professional judgment, taking into account the precise combination of circumstances in each individual instance. They will also need, on occasions, a little bit of luck, and sometimes they will make a wrong decision. Our Report emphasises the importance of teachers being able to discuss mistakes and difficulties openly with colleagues in an atmosphere of mutual support, rather than agonising about them in isolation.

Our support for training should not be seen as an assumption that discipline is some kind of optional extra, as if it were some sophisticated device which can transform a class in much the same way as a car wash transforms a grubby car. Discipline, and the development of self-discipline, cannot be separated from the total educational experience to which pupils are exposed in schools. Indeed, many aspects of indiscipline arise as direct responses by pupils to the experience of being taught.

Pupils are less likely to disrupt lessons which they see as interesting, relevant and worthwhile. They are more likely to disrupt those which they see as lifeless, boring or beyond their understanding. The implications for discipline of having an inappropriate or inadequately resourced curriculum, or one which is poorly presented, are obvious (and in some quarters we have been much chided with stating the obvious) but we hope that teachers will remember that our report was intended for a wider audience, to some of whom such thoughts may come as a surprise.

It was not, of course, part of our task to attempt to write a textbook on effective teaching, especially at a time when other committees are at work devising the National Curriculum, but we did make specific comments on three issues: the value of multi-cultural education, the need for the National Curriculum to make provision for personal and social education and the crucial importance of ensuring that the content of the National Curriculum, especially in the last years of compulsory schooling, is devised with the capabilities of the less academic and potentially disruptive pupils clearly in mind. If this last requirement is not met, and if the various alternative curricula now being used with such pupils are excluded, I would expect the National Curriculum to have an adverse effect on school discipline.

Of course, school discipline is not solely an issue confined to the classroom. It permeates the whole life of a school. It is for that reason that the most important part of our Report is concerned with the development, in each school, of a whole school behaviour policy. We feel that such policies should emphasise the positive encouragement of good behaviour, provide opportunities for teaching it and arrange for desirable behaviour to be recognised and rewarded. Regrettably, but realistically, it will also be necessary to set down certain prohibitions and punishments.

If a whole-school behaviour policy is to succeed it will need to be tailor-made to the precise requirements of the individual school. That is why it can only be devised by those who have inside knowledge of the school's life and work. It will also need to be rational and intelligible to all the people involved and the whole-school community will need to give willing support to its precepts and try to live by them. That end is not likely to be achieved if the policy is seen as something imposed from on high. The policy needs to evolve through a process of wide consultation with teachers, ancillary staff, pupils, parents and governors all feeling that their views have been heard, fairly considered and incorporated. In that way the whole-school behaviour policy ought to secure a wide measure of support.

No one can pretend that creating a consensus on discipline in this way is a simple management task for headteachers. Schools have to come to terms with so many new developments (the National Curriculum, national testing, teacher evaluation, profiling, GCSE and local financial management) that they may well think that the consultation process for arriving at whole-school behaviour policies simply cannot be fitted in. We hope, however, that they will come to recognise the contribution which a suitably devised and well-supported policy could make to the establishment of the kind of school ethos one finds in the most effective schools; an ethos in which everyone involved knows where they stand, what is expected of them, what is unacceptable and where to turn to for help when it is needed.

That last point brings me to the crucial question of support for the classroom teacher and for schools with serious problems. With the best will in the world it would be impossible to envisage teaching strategies or school policies which will not, from time to time, generate confrontations with uncooperative, disenchanted, violent, abusive, rebellious or anti-social pupils (or their parents). Many teachers complain bitterly that they are not properly backed up when they find themselves involved with problems of this kind. Indeed, this lack of confidence that their authority will be supported appears to be one of the commonest causes of low morale within the profession.

Our Committee felt strongly that the legal basis of the teachers' authority needs to be more clearly defined than it is at present, since it appears to rest on a confusing network of legal precedents, some more than a century old. It is difficult to see how teachers can exercise authority with any confidence when even lawyers differ about the legal basis of that authority. This can be a particularly difficult problem in such matters as truancy, detention, school dress, homework and the behaviour of pupils off the school premises.

Happily, most school discipline matters never come before the courts, and our Report emphasises the importance of teachers being more effectively supported in their day to day problems, both by their own peer group and by senior colleagues. We also stress the value of involving the great majority of parents who share the teachers' concern that their children shall behave in acceptable ways.

On the question of teachers who become the victims of violence in schools we have no hesitation in urging the fullest support from the police, the Crown Prosecution Service, the courts, and the LEAs in trying to ensure that every assistance is given to those who wish to pursue the legal remedies open to them. We also think that those who employ teachers should make proper provision for sympathetic counselling and financial compensation where appropriate.

We have asked that a national system for reporting serious incidents should be set up as quickly as possible. This should produce clear evidence of the nature, extent and location of serious indiscipline in schools. I would hope that those in charge of the education service would act on that evidence, wherever it might lead. If extra resources, panic buttons, security guards, modifications to buildings, additional teachers or courses in self-defence are shown to be necessary in some places, I hope that those responsible for the education service would recognise it to be their clear duty to provide them. Certainly teachers should not be expected to submit meekly to assaults from any quarter and our Report directs attention to the fact that teachers are still entitled, by law, to use reasonable force in defence of themselves, their pupils or school property.

We have urged that LEAs should ensure that they are able to offer a range of support services which can respond promptly when schools feel that they need specialist help and advice. LEA advisors, education welfare officers, the school psychological service and off-site units all have important roles to play in helping to improve school discipline but I do not underestimate the problems involved in persuading those who hold the purse strings to provide adequate resources for these support services. Nor do I underestimate the patience needed to establish the kind of climate in which both the requesting and offering of support can take place with confidence and goodwill on all sides. Grant-maintained schools will, presumably, be expected to 'buy in' specialist support if they require it and I hope they will be able to resist the temptation to off-load their problem pupils onto neighbouring schools still under LEA control.

In conclusion I should, perhaps, explain that we are optimistic about the kinds of improvement in school discipline which can be brought about because the kind of positive approaches which we advocate are already being successfully practised in schools, sometimes in very difficult areas.

Sadly, we have to acknowledge that some pupils will behave in such a violent or disruptive fashion that they have to be excluded from school, in fairness to other pupils and to the teachers and, sometimes, in their own best interests. Teachers should not use that sanction lightly and in most cases they take such decisions with great reluctance. We urge that those who have the power to over-rule the teachers' judgments in these cases should use that power very sparingly indeed, because re-admissions brought about in this way are damaging to staff morale and are unlikely to produce beneficial results. Full details of all such cases should be supplied to the Secretary of State.

Our Report examines the issue of exclusion in some detail and there is clearly a need for further experiment to discover effective means of meeting the educational needs of these very difficult pupils. They will not disappear. They will grow into adults. They will become parents in their turn and the education service cannot just wash its hands of them, for it may still be possible (if expensive) to teach them how to behave responsibly and how to respect the rights of other people.

REFERENCE

DES (1989) *Discipline in Schools (The Elton Report)*, London: HMSO.

2 Teacher training and classroom discipline

Frank Merrett and Kevin Wheldall

A common expectation among young people going to a college, poly-technic or a university department to prepare for a career in teaching is that they will be taught how to teach. In reality, students tend to be taught a great deal about the content of syllabuses and the planning of lessons but the business of bringing about successful learning outcomes or how to manage a class is rarely addressed. The only time that students come into contact with teachers and the teaching process is on teaching practice. The oppor-tunities for learning the skills of teaching on teaching practice are largely dependent upon luck. Some schools welcome students and some teachers are very understanding and helpful. Some pupils are prepared to make allowances for beginners and some supervisors are skilled, have recent and appropriate experience and are interested in helping their students learn to cope. The chance of a student finding all, or even most, of these variables in his or her favour are uncertain. Consequently, even a period of practical teaching may not facilitate the learning of appropriate skills either.

Conversations with practising teachers suggest that what students expected most of all from their courses, they did not receive. Most of them anticipated that by the end of their preparation they would have learned something about how human beings learn new skills and acquire new information. They expected to be in possession of techniques and skills that would enable them to manage groups of children and to bring about good learning outcomes. They expected to be given opportunities to practise these in meaningful contexts and to receive expert coaching from estab-lished, successful practitioners. Rarely were these expectations met.

The experience of some teachers is particularly bad. Cross, a student teacher in the late 1970s, thought so badly about his professional education that he wrote these words to the *Observer* newspaper in 1983:

> We spent a great deal of time learning theory and ideology....Discipline was an ugly word at college, although our everyday teaching is affected

and possibly shaped by it. Not once in three years was it discussed. How should one react if a child refuses to do what he is told? What if a child swears at you? How do you establish silence? What forms of punishment should be used?...For me three years at college were a waste of time. When I began my first teaching post it was like stepping into a different world – which I was ill-equipped to deal with. Training college had been just a way of gaining a certificate.

A large number of researchers has investigated the feelings of teachers about the process of learning to become teachers and many have found grave anxieties among students especially in the area of classroom management (Zeidner, 1988; Putnam, 1985; Hart, 1987; Kremer-Hayon and Ben-Peretz, 1986; Veenman, 1987; Selkirk, 1988; Sandys, 1988). HMI in two recent Reports (DES, 1982; 1988) have reported on teachers in their probationary year and have commented on the large proportion who seem to be ill-prepared, especially in the area of classroom behaviour management.

The Elton Report (DES, 1989) was concerned about many of the same issues commented upon in the earlier surveys. The general issue of classroom behaviour management came under the scrutiny of the Committee of Enquiry. The Report refers to 'group management skills' which includes the ability to relate to young people, to encourage them in good behaviour and learning, and to deal calmly but firmly with inappropriate or disruptive behaviour. The Report comments,

> Our evidence suggests that the importance of group management skills tends to be underestimated by teachers and their trainers. This was confirmed by our expert witnesses. We find this worrying because it is an area of competence which relates most directly to pupil behaviour.
>
> (DES, 1989, p.67)

The Report also suggests that whilst some people appear to be natural teachers, the majority can become more effective classroom managers as the result of the right kinds of training, experience and support (ibid., 14, p.69). It goes on to state that,

> The beliefs that either group management skills should not be necessary or that they cannot be learned seem to be traditional in parts of the profession.

The Committee of Enquiry contacted all 105 LEAs in England and Wales and found that most of them do not provide in-service training in classroom behaviour management. They found this surprising in view of the fact that three out of four teachers in their survey felt that more training in this area was needed. Consequently the Report concluded,

Our evidence leads us to three important conclusions. First, that teachers' group management skills are probably the single most important factor in achieving good standards of classroom behaviour. Second, that those skills can be taught and learned. Third, that practical training provision in this area is inadequate.

The Report goes on to make suggestions for improvement and commended action on the part of training establishments and LEAs which included applying the principles of good classroom management, more specific initial training, more specific in-service training and better induction programmes for new teachers.

The DES Circular 24/89 on 'Initial teacher training: approval of courses' has clearly taken on board some of the recommendations of the Elton Report. Section 6.5 of Annexe A states:

> All courses should contain compulsory and clearly identifiable elements of practical training which will help develop in students skills in the effective management of pupil behaviour. Such training should include specific, institution based elements on the acquisition of group management techniques.

(p.10)

In the commentary in section 9, in Annexe B, the document further states:

> Students should learn the importance of classroom management and different models of classroom organisation. Students should be able, on completion of the course, to manage children individually, in groups and as a whole class so that work is carried out in a responsible and orderly manner.

(p.20)

THE WEST MIDLANDS STUDY

We decided to obtain a database of opinion from a representative sample of teachers in secondary schools in the West Midlands to see how far they felt that their initial training had prepared them for the problems they had to face in their classrooms. Since the return rates for questionnaire surveys are so variable and unpredictable we decided to carry out this investigation by means of structured interviews. A structured interview schedule was devised and used in a pilot study with fifty secondary teachers chosen at random from the staffs of seven schools in the West Midlands. After careful scrutiny of the results several small amendments and additions were made to the schedule in preparation for the main study.

No names were entered on the interview schedule form but the interviewer used a panel at the top to identify schools and teachers and to note the sex of the teacher responding. The first questions were framed so as to gain information about the teachers' professional qualifications, the type of institutions at which these qualifications had been gained, the number of years of teaching service and their subject specialisms. The first substantive question asked 'Do you think that your initial course of training gave you sufficient preparation in terms of (a) curriculum content, (b) the educational system, (c) classroom behaviour management, (d) special educational needs and (e) child development. The next question asked about the importance to teachers of the ability to manage (control) a class whilst question seven asked teachers where they had learned to manage a class. They were asked whether they had gained these skills during their teacher training course and if so, how; or whether they had learned 'on the job'. Those who had answered affirmatively to the earlier question were then asked if they thought this training in classroom management to have been effective. The next two questions were concerned with matters of order and control, first asking teachers whether they felt that they spent too much time on such matters and then asking a similar question relating to their colleagues. Next they were asked whether they agreed that it is better to be positive and encouraging towards children in class rather than to nag and chide and then whether they thought that they, themselves, were positive. The following questions asked whether they had heard about the behavioural approach to teaching (or positive teaching) and whether, if a course to help them to be more positive in their classroom management was on offer, they would be willing to attend. The next question was concerned with the likely outcomes of training in classroom management and asked whether teachers thought that it would help to reduce stress among teachers, help to reduce troublesome behaviour among pupils and third, whether it would help newly qualified teachers. The last two questions sought information about what pupil behaviours teachers found to be most troublesome and how far they had been subjected to physical violence and verbal abuse by their pupils during the course of their careers so far.

The amendments made to the structured interview schedule were so trivial that it seemed reasonable to collapse the data from the pilot study (fifty teachers) and the main study (126 teachers) and report the results from the two surveys together where, as in most cases, the questions were exactly the same. Thus, the schedule was used to obtain data on 176 teachers in twenty-one secondary schools chosen randomly from local authority lists of schools in the West Midlands. The headteachers of the schools were contacted by letter and most responded by agreeing to take part in the study; only three refused to co-operate. Teachers taking part were selected arbitrarily by headteachers from the nominal list of staff members, so providing a reasonably random selection of respondents. No teacher selected to take part actually refused to do so.

Of the 176 teachers in this (combined) sample ninety were men and eighty-six were women. Eighty-two were certificated teachers, fifty-four had a post-graduate teaching qualification, twenty-nine had a B.Ed. qualification, five had Diplomas in Education whilst six others had some other teaching qualification. The institutions attended included colleges of education, university departments of education, polytechnics, colleges of higher education and a technical college. The mean length of service of the teachers was just over fourteen years. As might be expected, the range of subject areas taught by these teachers was very wide. The humanities (history, geography, etc.), science subjects, mathematics, P.E., English and other languages were all well represented. Others taught art, craft, design and technology, home economics, information technology, business studies, drama, economics, music and religious education, whilst some were concerned with children with special educational needs.

The first question asked for teachers' opinions and views on the preparation their initial course had given them about a number of educational issues. Data were available for 123 teachers. The first of these issues was curriculum content and 51 per cent of respondents found their preparation in this area sufficient. Second was how children develop and learn, in this area 78 per cent were satisfied with their initial courses. Third was the educational system, how it operates and who is there to help teachers, 68 per cent of the sample thought that their preparation was unsatisfactory. Fourth was classroom behaviour management, here 72 per cent of the teachers were dissatisfied with the preparation they were given. Finally, with regard to teaching children with special needs, 75 per cent felt insufficiently prepared.

The next question asked about the importance to teachers of being able to manage a class. Respondents were given a choice of five answers varying from 'very important' through 'important' to 'of no importance at all'. A small number thought it important whilst all the rest thought it very important. This leaves no room for doubt at all that in the minds of teachers, classroom behaviour management is a matter of prime importance.

The following question attempted to find out where teachers felt they had learned their skills of classroom behaviour management. Eighteen per cent of teachers believed that they had learned these skills during their initial training but the rest (82 per cent) thought that they had had to learn them 'on the job'. Of those who believed that they had learned to manage a class in college, most thought that this had been through supervised teaching practice.

The next two questions related to the time teachers spend on matters of order and control. Thirty-eight per cent of teachers believed that too much of their time was taken up with these issues. When the same question was asked relating to their colleagues, there was a complete shift in the balance of responses. Nearly three-quarters answered 'yes', that their colleagues were spending too much time on disciplinary matters.

All but one of the teachers in this survey of opinion believed that it is better to be positive and encouraging towards children rather than to be constantly scolding and nagging. Ninety-six per cent thought that they, themselves, were, on the whole, more positive than negative. Seventy-four per cent of teachers had heard of the behavioural approach to teaching and 83 per cent said that they would be prepared to attend a course on positive classroom behaviour management if one were on offer.

The next question related to the possible outcomes of training in classroom behaviour management. Of this sample of teachers, 82 per cent believed that such a course would reduce stress among their colleagues. Sixty-seven per cent believed that a course in positive classroom behaviour management would help to reduce the level of pupil misbehaviour. On the effect of such a course on newly qualified teachers there was a greater measure of agreement. Ninety-two per cent believed that such a course would help new teachers to cope during their first year of teaching.

In the following question teachers were asked to identify the type of pupil behaviour that bothers them most in their teaching. This question was, unlike most of the others, completely open-ended so the results were difficult to analyse. An attempt was made to categorise the results which showed that lack of motivation (including apathy, lethargy, failure to carry out instructions) and talking out of turn were cited most frequently, followed by lack of manners/rudeness and inattentiveness. Other comments included lack of respect for authority, under-achievement, lack of concentration, disaffection, hindering other pupils, noise and so on, but only one teacher mentioned violence (and this was a reference to the *possibility* of violence) and only one mentioned aggression.

The last question related to personal experience of physical violence and verbal abuse. A very large proportion of teachers (82 per cent) reported that they had never been subjected to physical violence during their teaching careers. A much larger proportion of this sample of teachers reported having been subjected to verbal abuse with 75 per cent answering 'yes'.

CONCLUSIONS

Research based on the results of questionnaires or material gained from interviews such as these must always be interpreted with care. Opinions given in such circumstances may not always be reliable. Some people have not really thought about the questions put before them, some may be trying to impress and some give the answers they think that the interviewer is expecting. Nevertheless, in this case, the people being asked were giving opinions about issues central to their professional work and based upon personal experience, in some cases over many years.

The principal finding from this investigation is that teachers regard the ability to control a class as a matter of prime importance. All but a small minority of the teachers interviewed agreed that it is very important and the rest thought that it is important. This belief is reflected in the literature where many reports mention the fears of new teachers and the anxiety caused to experienced teachers by discipline problems. This was also, of course, one of the main findings of the Elton Report.

The second important fact that is underlined by this study is that whatever is being done in training institutions to tackle this problem has not been working very well. Teachers clearly believed that the training they had received had not prepared them sufficiently for classroom behaviour management and that they had had to learn to manage a class 'on the job'.

The number of teachers admitting to spending more time than they ought on matters of class control was much lower than in earlier surveys (Houghton *et al.*, 1988; see Chapter 6). The reason for this is probably that these data come from face-to-face interviews whereas the earlier data had come from anonymous questionnaires. Some teachers do not realise that they have problems and of those that do it takes a great deal of courage to recognise the fact and own up, even to oneself. It takes a great deal more to write it down and even more to admit it to an interviewer. Most teachers were only too willing to admit, however, that their colleagues had problems in this area!

In this study teachers were asked to say how satisfied they were with certain aspects of their initial professional course. Seventy per cent or more were not satisfied with those aspects of the courses which dealt with the structure of the educational system, with meeting the needs of children with special problems and with classroom behaviour management. These figures, in the main, reflect the content of training courses of some years ago because not many of the sample were beginners. The recent reports of HMI referred to earlier suggest lower figures and this might indicate that training is better now than it was. The data were examined to see whether this was the case. No discernible differences were to be noted when these data were analysed by length of service. For those above the upper quartile and for those below the lower quartile about one-third were satisfied with their training. For the intermediate groups about one-fifth expressed satisfaction. There was no trend.

The vast majority of teachers agreed that to be encouraging is better than to be severe and repressive with children and this is a finding that is itself very encouraging and optimistic. Nearly all the teachers thought that they were more positive in their approach to their pupils than negative. This does not match closely with the findings of one of our observational studies carried out to examine this point (Wheldall *et al.*, 1989; see Chapter 6). In this study 130 secondary teachers were observed at work with their own classes and data were collected on the number of positive and negative comments given by the teachers to their pupils. For academic behaviour, positive responses were three times as frequent as negative responses but for social behaviour, negative responses were three times as frequent as positive responses. Teachers know that in order to get the best work out of children it is necessary to be encouraging and on the whole they are. But, typically, they expect their pupils to behave well and when this happens, they do not find it necessary to comment. However, when they behave badly they feel forced to act and usually do so. The kinds of actions they resort to on these occasions do not appear to be very effective to judge by the responses of teachers about the time they spend on matters of order and control. Some teachers are very negative whilst some do not give much feedback at all.

- The majority of teachers questioned had heard of behavioural approaches to teaching or 'positive teaching'. This is an approach to teaching which commends positiveness and which trains teachers in positive ways of improving classroom behaviour management (Wheldall and Merrett, 1989; Merrett and Wheldall, 1990). About 80 per cent of teachers said that they would be prepared to attend a course in such methods if it were on offer. The Elton Report (DES, 1989) has commended such courses and made strong recommendations that both at initial training and at the in-service level, opportunities should be provided for teachers to receive such training. Teachers, generally, are clearly interested in courses of this nature which they believe will improve their management skills which, as this investigation has shown, is of great importance to them. The effects of such training were seen by teachers in this survey as being very beneficial, particularly in the reduction of teacher stress. A very high proportion of the teachers believed that such courses would be of particular benefit to teachers at the start of their careers.

It is strange that issues which are manifestly of prime importance to practising teachers should receive so little attention from the people who are engaged in initial training courses for teachers. The answers to the questions about the length of time teachers believe that they and their colleagues are having to give to matters of order and control are very revealing and suggest that disciplinary issues bulk large in the stress and anxiety felt by many teachers. Most teachers thought that their colleagues spent more time than they ought on matters of order and control. The evidence on which these opinions are based is difficult to determine but teachers get a 'nose' for what is going on in adjoining classrooms after a time and much comes from staffroom conversational exchanges.

The data which came from the answers to the question about the sorts of behaviour teachers find most troublesome were difficult to analyse since the responses were so various. Generally, the answers given tended to be descriptions of broad classes of response which would probably best be described as inferred attitudes rather than behaviours *per se*. Nevertheless, two facts are clear. The kinds of behaviour that teachers found most troublesome were not of a serious nature and violence and aggression were mentioned hardly at all. These findings are very similar to those of Houghton *et al*., (1988; see Chapter 6) and of the research commissioned by the Elton Committee and carried out from the University of Sheffield (DES, 1989).

The Elton Committee commented on the fact that the 'group management skills' which they themselves regarded as of prime importance seem to be little regarded by teacher trainers. This assumption is accompanied by the belief that such skills cannot be learned. This was clearly not the belief of those who wrote *Discipline in Schools* and it is to be hoped that the advice given to the DES and which has been underlined and supported by the Secretary of State will be heeded. Money has been made available for in-service training and it will be interesting to see whether those in control of teacher education in this country will seize their opportunity. In order to do so many will have to undergo a complete change of heart and mind. If such methods were not proscribed by positive teaching, the method advocated by Richard Nixon in his oft-quoted remark is tempting in this context. Then, perhaps, 'their hearts and minds would follow'!

REFERENCES

Cross, J. (1983) The *Observer*, 13 March.
DES (1982) *The New Teacher in School: a survey by Her Majesty's Inspectors in England and Wales 1981*, London: HMSO.
—— (1988) *The New Teacher in School: a survey by Her Majesty's Inspectors in England and Wales 1987*, London: HMSO.
—— (1989) *Discipline in Schools (The Elton Report)*, London: HMSO.

Hart, N.I. (1987) 'Students teachers' anxieties: four measured factors and their relationships to pupil disruption in class', *Educational Research* 29: 12–18.

Houghton, S., Wheldall, K. and Merrett, F. (1988) 'Classroom behaviours which secondary school teachers say they find most troublesome', *British Educational Research Journal* 14: 295–310.

Kremer-Hayon, L. and Ben-Peretz, M. (1986) 'Becoming a teacher: the transition from teachers' college to classroom life', *International Review of Education* 32: 413–22.

Merrett, F. and Wheldall, K. (1990) *Positive Teaching in the Primary School*, London: Paul Chapman.

Putnam, J.G. (1985) 'Applications of classroom management research findings', *Journal of Education for Teaching* 11: 145–64.

Sandys, E.J.A. (1988) 'Teachers' perceptions of the issues', in *Alternative Approaches to Children with Behaviour and Emotional Difficulties*, Edinburgh: Scottish Education Department.

Selkirk, E. (1988) 'Teachers' needs for training in classroom behaviour management', in *Alternative Approaches to Children with Behaviour and Emotional Difficulties*, Edinburgh: Scottish Education Department.

Veenman, S. (1987) 'Problems as perceived by new teachers', in N. Hastings and J. Schwieso (eds) *New Directions in Educational Psychology 2: Behaviour and motivation in the classroom*, London: Falmer.

Wheldall, K. and Merrett, M. (1989) *Positive Teaching in the Secondary School*, London: Paul Chapman.

Wheldall, K., Houghton, S. and Merrett, F. (1989) 'Natural rates of teacher approval and disapproval in British secondary school classrooms', *British Journal of Educational Psychology* 59: 38–48.

Zeidner, M. (1988) 'The relative severity of common classroom management strategies: the student's perspective', *British Journal of Educational Psychology* 58: 69–77.

3 Discipline is for the whole school

Ted Glynn

Successful behaviour management and disciplinary practices in a school require a school-wide policy and commitment. It is good to see the Elton Report (DES, 1989) acknowledge and endorse this view. In what follows, I will try to draw out some of the practical implications of a whole-school approach to discipline and behaviour management. There are important implications in this Report concerning changes in staff behaviour towards pupils which are required of such a team approach. There are also implications concerning the school curriculum, concerning relationships with parents and concerning the integration (mainstreaming) of children who have special needs. Not all of these implications appear to be fully appreciated in the Report. I would like to comment on each area in turn. My comments are based on my research and experience in the development of within-school support systems for children with behavioural and learning difficulties in New Zealand (Thomas and Glynn, 1976; Thomas *et al.*, 1977; Glynn *et al.*, 1978; Glynn *et al.*, 1983).

A TEAM APPROACH TO BEHAVIOUR MANAGEMENT AND DISCIPLINE

The Elton Report is correct, I believe, in pointing out that developing and implementing a school policy on behaviour management requires a major commitment of time and resources. This includes positive and active leadership from the headteacher and senior staff. The Report also calls for the appointment of a facilitator, from within the school staff, who will be responsible for the development and monitoring of staff training. Being an insider, this facilitator will be in a better and stronger position than a peripatetic visitor to gain and hold the trust and confidence of school staff. However, this facilitator will need to be seen to be selected for his or her own competence and strengths in teaching and in behaviour management. He or she will need sufficient status within the school to influence staff behaviour and effect change throughout the school, perhaps including change in more senior colleagues. This is a very daunting remit.

Together, the team comprising headteacher, senior staff and facilitator will need to arrange a series of discussions involving all staff in the formulation of school policy. Producing a negotiated agreement on school rules and the graduated series of staff responses to pupil behaviour as called for in the Report will not be easy. This process will be a new experience for many teachers. Many will be challenged to find that their colleagues hold quite different views from themselves about what constitutes acceptable behaviour in the classroom or playground. What some teachers consider mildly inappropriate swearing, others may consider an intolerable and unacceptable affront to their authority. Some will regard pupil complaints about unreasonable school rules as a starting point for negotiation. Others will regard such behaviour as insubordinate and disrespectful. Yet all these differences must be aired, confronted and resolved before there can be any serious attempt at reaching consensus on staff responses to pupil behaviour. In my experience, such a negotiated agreement may require several lengthy discussion meetings extending over several weeks or months (Glynn *et al.*, 1983; Pluck *et al.*, 1987). Headteacher involvement and support will be essential.

There are other implications for the implementation of school policy on behaviour management and discipline. Good behaviour management requires regular and frequent positive feedback on performance. How often do schools provide positive feedback for pupils who are regular school attenders? What feedback is there for children who complete two, four, six or eight weeks without a single incident of disruptive or aggressive behaviour? What feedback is there for a whole class of children among whom there has been no fighting for a whole school term? There is more to a positive behaviour management policy than producing explicit rules which are positively stated. Schools, it seems, can publicly display graphs and figures concerning details of fund raising ventures and sporting achievements. Do they publicly display and comment on their progress towards achieving positive *social* behaviour goals? How much emphasis is given in assemblies, in staff meetings and in classrooms to discussion of the attainment of social behaviour goals? Research cited in Wheldall and Glynn (1989) demonstrates that while teachers explicitly target and reinforce appropriate academic behaviour goals, they merely expect that appropriate social behaviour will happen. There is a great deal of work to be done in school policy making in this area.

There are further requirements also. Given that a school has successfully reached agreement on acceptable pupil behaviour and on a graduated series of staff responses to unacceptable pupil behaviour, these responses need to be written down, explicitly modelled and specifically taught. This opens up a major skills training agenda for the in-service training of all teachers. (This is particularly important given the general lack of behaviour management training in pre-service teacher education identified by the authors of the Elton Report.) Such an agenda might include learning to deliver clear and concise instructions and directions, learning to negotiate disagreements and conflicts, learning to respond to pupils' initiations and learning to promote pupil self-management and responsibility for pupils' own behaviour. Paradoxically, self control and self-management skills may be learned best in the context of social interaction with others (Risley, 1977). Staff behaviour is therefore critical. Pupils are unlikely to learn autonomy and independence in the context of totally controlling and directive behaviour of school staff.

Senior staff and facilitators will need to have easy access to outside professionals in these skill areas. In New Zealand, educational psychologists are trained to take leadership roles in these areas of in-service training. However, outside professionals must work in consultation with and through each school's teacher/facilitator. Each school must own its in-service training programme and accept responsibility for its implementation. This is not the sole responsibility of the outside consultant.

Adopting this style of approach to behaviour management will bring to the surface even more practical concerns. Staff will need and want to observe their colleagues in action in their classrooms. This will present major organisational challenges. Some staff will be defensive about their colleagues observing them. Many will be reluctant to gather or share information about their own behaviour. Many will be decidedly uncomfortable about receiving feedback on their own behaviour or about giving feedback to their colleagues. Yet, performance feedback on one's own behaviour is well established as an essential component of behaviour change in staff training programmes (Glynn and Vaigro, 1984). The role of headteacher, senior staff and facilitator in implementing in-service training in behaviour management is indeed a daunting one.

CURRICULUM ISSUES

The Report identifies personal and social education as an important component of good behaviour management. I strongly endorse this. However, like the authors of the Report, I note that the status of personal and social education is no longer clear in the context of the development of the National Curriculum. It seems unreasonable for government and society to continue to make demands that schools ensure pupils meet expected standards of personal and social behaviour, without making explicit provision for this in the National Curriculum. The rate of social change and the complexities and stresses of living in Britain and Europe render it critical that schools provide opportunities for pupils to learn social and interpersonal skills. These skills should include those of advocating change, negotiating and resolving conflict, as well as ways of changing one's own behaviour. Such skills have major implications for diet, exercise, fitness and mental health as well as for learning academic and social behaviour. Where better to learn these skills than in the context of the social life of the school itself?

A sound personal and social education curriculum would link itself to school policy on behaviour management and discipline. The Report acknowledges that pupils behave more responsibly when given responsibility. Why not permit pupil input into the process of formulating this policy? Pupils can contribute a great deal to identifying and specifying appropriate rewards and sanctions and, as two recent research studies have shown, they can come up with some surprisingly concrete and practical suggestions (Sharpe *et al.*, 1987; Houghton *et al.*, 1988).

Why not establish a mechanism by which they can offer constructive criticism and constructive suggestions for solving some of the behaviour problems they experience (Glynn, 1976)? This may reduce some of the disruptive behaviour arising from being powerless to change a system which imposes inconsistent and arbitrary sanctions on one's academic and social behaviour.

At the level of individual behaviour change, why not encourage teachers and pupils to negotiate explicit behaviour contracts, requiring each to modify their behaviour with respect to the other and to subject their contract to monitoring by a third party? Of course, professional consultation is required with this process, lest the contract be simply imposed unilaterally upon a reluctant pupil by a controlling and autocratic teacher.

However, personal and social education is not the only route into the school curriculum for behaviour management and discipline. The broad sphere of the social sciences is another. Why not establish a school-wide behaviour change project? This could involve identifying a specific management problem, gathering objective and systematic data, devising a strategy for change, implementing that strategy and evaluating its effectiveness throughout the school. Two New Zealand research studies described in Glynn and McNaughton (1978) bear on this suggestion. The first examined fighting and disruptive behaviour in the playground of an urban school, an area of concern identified by the Elton Report. O'Rourke and Glynn (1978) demonstrated that marked improvement in children's playground behaviour, and a marked reduction in playground fighting occurred when teachers and other adults moved about starting up games and activities to engage more and more children, instead of merely patrolling and supervising. This study also found that the number of fights varied systematically according to which teams of teachers were on playground duty. These findings strongly support the case for a consistent school-wide approach to behaviour management.

The second study (Presland, 1978) was concerned with reducing the amount of litter deposited in the school playground. A team of pupils partitioned the playground into ten zones and collected baseline data on the amount of litter deposited daily in each zone. The school provided systematic positive feedback in the form of large display graphs, depicting the gradual reduction of the amount of litter deposited. The feedback was introduced successively, first in two or three zones, and then into more and more zones, once the feedback procedure had been established as effective.

I see no reason why a class or school social science project could not apply these strategies to a variety of behaviour management problems, for example, school attendance, late arrival for classes, lunchroom behaviour, care of school equipment and assessing how providing fitted carpets might reduce classroom noise levels and amount of work completed. Pupils would benefit from gaining knowledge and experience in applying empirical procedures to human behaviour and in understanding some of the variables which are strong enough to change human behaviour. Pupils would benefit also from working collaboratively with staff to solve a human behaviour problem in which they each have a considerable stake.

RELATIONSHIPS WITH PARENTS

In this area, the Report is somewhat one-sided. It clearly advocates better and more frequent school–home communication. It is concerned that parents receive explicit and detailed information about the school's behaviour management and discipline policy. It is concerned that parents be contacted very early in the chain of events when things begin to go wrong for their child. It is concerned that parents receive positive information about their children's successes and improvements. I can only endorse these concerns heartily. However, the Report goes further than this. It advocates increased accountability of parents for the behaviour of their children while they are at school (for example, it discusses making parents liable for damage caused by their children). It seeks clarification of teachers' authority in their own right as teachers, noting that the principle *in loco parentis* is no longer adequate. It seeks to clarify teachers' authority to set homework and to impose punishments.

For me, movement in this direction raises some important issues. If parents are to be held increasingly responsible for what their children do at school, ought there to be some mechanism by which parents can influence what is done to their children at school? If my child damages a piece of school property or equipment in frustration because she has been humiliated or harassed by other children, or because she has been unjustly punished for some act, am I to be held responsible? If my previous attempts to express my concern about anti-social behaviour in the playground or classroom have been brushed aside as being evidence of my over-protection, or worse, interference, ought I now to be held responsible? Moves to formalise teacher authority may result in new or increased attempts by parents to establish greater control over what happens to their children at school. Such a unilateral approach to clarifying teacher authority will work against teacher–parent partnership and shared responsibilities and may undermine mutual respect and trust which teachers and parents should have for each other (Blackstone, 1979).

I believe better teacher–parent working relationships will result from teachers and parents working together. Just as increased pupil responsibility is seen as arising from giving pupils more responsibilities, so too will increased parent responsibility arise from giving parents more responsibilities. Exercising these responsibilities will be extremely difficult for parents whose community language and culture is not English and for parents of children with behaviour and learning difficulties. Past experiences of these parents with the school system are likely to have been aversive. But a whole-school approach to behaviour management and discipline must grapple with this issue. Parental consultation and input is essential. At present almost all the power in the teacher–parent relationship lies with teachers. Hence initiatives for power sharing must begin with teachers.

INTEGRATION OF CHILDREN WITH SPECIAL NEEDS

The Report suggests that the most effective provision for pupils with emotional and behavioural difficulties is likely to be based on support teams of specialist teachers working in mainstream schools. I strongly endorse this position. There is not space to do justice to the range of literature advocating the mainstreaming of all children with special needs. The UNESCO *Consultation on Special Education Action for Disabled Persons* (UNESCO, 1988), and Education systems in Canada, the USA, and to an increased extent Australia and New Zealand, are stressing as a basic human right, the right of all individual children, regardless of degree of disability or handicap, to receive an education appropriate to their needs at their local school along with their own peer group.

Consistent with this ethical position, delivery of services for children with special needs should take place via their full participation in a regular class at their local school. Withdrawal into special classrooms or units, or withdrawal from their classrooms for extended individual instruction is not mainstreaming in this sense. Ballard (1988) cites Canadian and US research as showing that any such withdrawal creates islands in the mainstream. These islands ensure that the mainstream of education in the school, its teachers, its teaching methods, its curriculum and its assessment and evaluation practices all remain unchanged and unaffected by the presence of children who have special needs. Instead, Ballard advocates total inclusion of special needs children in all the activities of the regular classroom. Only this degree of participation, 100 per cent, he argues, will result in the necessary changes occurring in teacher and child attitude and behaviour and in modifications to the regular class curriculum to support the inclusion of children who have special needs. Wider adoption of methods such as co-operative teaching (Johnson and Johnson, 1979) and peer tutoring (Tavener and Glynn, 1989) may also result from including special needs children among their regular classroom peers.

A successful whole-school approach to behaviour management and discipline will make the mainstreaming of children who have special needs much easier. Classroom teachers, specialist teachers, parents and professional resource people will already be familiar with sharing responsibility and working together. Within such an approach, it will become increasingly difficult to justify excluding children who have disabilities or handicaps or who experience behavioural and learning difficulties. The need for high quality and effective in-service training for all teachers, in order to achieve these aims, cannot be overstated. The role of a team comprising the headteacher, senior staff and a teacher/facilitator in upgrading and monitoring the level of behaviour management and professional skills in their school will be crucial. Specialist and regular teachers can no longer afford to work in isolation from each other. The Elton Report does education a great service in taking this line. We are all responsible for what goes on in our schools.

REFERENCES

Ballard, K.D. (1988) 'Toward the non-restrictive environment', *The Exceptional Child Monograph* 1: 7–18.
Blackstone, T. (1979) 'Parental involvement in education', *Education Policy Bulletin* 7: 81–98.
DES (1989) *Discipline in Schools (The Elton Report)*, London: HMSO.
Glynn, E.L. (1976) 'Student behaviour: a self-management approach', in J.A. Codd

and G.L. Hermansson (eds) *Directions in New Zealand Secondary Education*, Auckland: Hodder & Stoughton.

Glynn, E.L., Thomas, J.D. and Wotherspoon, A.T. (1978) 'Applied psychology in the Mangere Guidance Unit: implementing behavioural services in the school', *The Exceptional Child* 25: 115–26.

Glynn, T. and McNaughton, S. (1978) (eds) *Applied Behaviour Analysis in New Zealand, 1978: proceedings of the first New Zealand conference for research in applied behaviour analysis*, Auckland: Education Department, University of Auckland.

Glynn, T. and Vaigro, W. (1984) 'Accountability through record keeping in a residential setting', *The Exceptional Child* 31: 142–50.

Glynn, T., Seymour, F., Robertson, A. and Bullen, D. (1983) 'Glenburn child behaviour management procedures', *Behavioural Approaches with Children* 7, 1: 17–32.

Houghton, S., Merrett, F. and Wheldall, K. (1988) 'The attitudes of British secondary school pupils to praise, rewards, punishments and reprimands: a further study', *New Zealand Journal of Educational Studies* 23: 223–34.

Johnson, D. and Johnson, R. (1979) 'Co-operative learning strategies for mainstreaming/integration', *S.E.T. Research Information for Teachers* 1, Item 4, Wellington: New Zealand Council for Educational Research.

O'Rourke, M. and Glynn, T. (1978) 'Play equipment and adult participation: effects on children's playground behaviour', in T. Glynn and S. McNaughton (eds) *Applied Behaviour Analysis in New Zealand 1978: proceedings of the first New Zealand conference for research in applied behaviour analysis*, Auckland: Education Department, University of Auckland.

Pluck, D., Glynn, T. and Strandring, D. (1987) 'Staff change: child change', *Journal of the New Zealand Psychological Service Association* 8: 27–34.

Presland, D. (1978) 'Procedures for litter removal in an intermediate school playground', in T. Glynn and S. McNaughton (eds) *Applied Behaviour Analysis in New Zealand 1978: proceedings of the first New Zealand conference for research in applied behaviour analysis*, Auckland: Education Department, University of Auckland.

Risley, T.R. (1977) 'The social context of self control', in B.R. Stuart (ed.) *Behavioural Self-management: strategies, techniques and outcome*, New York: Bruner/Mazel.

Sharpe, P., Wheldall, K. and Merrett, F. (1987) 'The attitudes of British secondary students towards praise', *Behavioural Approaches with Children* 9: 109–12.

Tavener, J. and Glynn, T. (1989) 'Peer tutoring as a context for children learning English as a second language', *Language and Education* (*in press*).

Thomas, J.D. and Glynn, E.L. (1976) *Mangere Guidance Unit: evaluation of behavioural programmes*, Report to the Director-General of Education, Wellington: Department of Education.

Thomas, J.D. and Pohl, F., Presland, I. and Glynn, E.L. (1977) 'A behaviour analysis approach to guidance', *New Zealand Journal of Educational Studies* 12: 17–28.

UNESCO (1988) *Consultation on Special Education Action for Disabled Persons*, Paris: UNESCO.

Wheldall, K. and Glynn, T. (1989) *Effective Classroom Learning*, Oxford: Basil Blackwell.

4 Keeping them clever: Preventing learning difficulties from becoming behaviour problems

Colin J. Smith

As the Elton Report (DES, 1989) points out, there is a danger that learning needs may be neglected if a pupil has been stereotyped as disruptive. The Report also acknowledges the difficulty in distinguishing the causes of low achievement:

> some pupils are low achievers because they lack the motivation to work in school, others because they lack the ability. For many both factors are at work.
>
> (DES, 1989, para. 4, p.73)

However, though there has long been an awareness of the interaction between intellectual and emotional factors, less attention has been given to an examination of how to prevent learning difficulties from becoming behaviour problems than to the consideration of how to cope with such problems once they have arisen.

Prevention is always considered to be better than cure but as far as disruptive behaviour is concerned, whilst thought is frequently given to the ways in which personal relations contribute to the climate and atmosphere of the classroom, less attention is paid to the part academic demands and expectations can play in promoting a positive or negative attitude to school life. As one pupil explained to Hargreaves (1967), one of his friends (renowned by this time as the dominant member of the fourth-year delinquent group) started his secondary-school life in the A stream but changed on being demoted to a lower stream. He would have remained 'all right' as Hargreaves' informant put it, if only the teachers had 'kept him clever'.

Many problems experienced with disaffected pupils could be avoided if schools were sufficiently adroit at 'keeping them clever'. Too often the messages conveyed by both overt and covert curricula are construed as offering little to pupils, who are excluded from certain courses or denied access to particular privileges. Such pupils may well respond by behaving in ways which convey a reciprocally antagonistic message. Children may ward off feelings of inadequacy by indulgence in misbehaviour, display indolence in order to disguise incompetence and assert a lack of concern so as to hide a lack of ability.

EXPECTATIONS

If schools have low expectations of their pupils, it cannot be surprising if pupils respond by living down to such expectations. Evans (1981) draws a pertinent distinction between 'insidious' and 'excessive' disruptive behaviour. The former is characterised by commonplace unpunctuality, failure to produce homework, turning up for lessons without necessary books or equipment, displaying open boredom and demonstrating unwillingness to concentrate on classroom tasks. Once such behaviour becomes the norm, it may foster an atmosphere conducive to more 'excessive' misbehaviour such as outright defiance, damage to property, persistent aggression and violent attacks on pupils or staff.

Sometimes teachers themselves may provide a poor example of respect for the values which they are notionally aiming to inculcate. If lessons start late and finish early, if work is set but not promptly marked, if anger is expressed through demeaning personal abuse and turns rapidly to physical intervention, then it is likely that pupils themselves will acquire a disdain for punctuality and perseverance and respond to provocation with uncontrolled hostility. On the other hand, good models of teacher behaviour exhibiting commitment, concern and personal respect, set standards which reflect positive expectations of pupil behaviour and attainment.

Clear effective definition and feedback on what is acceptable conduct is another key feature of the ethos of successful schools identified in research studies by Rutter *et al.*, (1979); Mortimore *et al.*, (1988) and others considered in the Elton Report (DES, 1989). There is indeed strong evidence to support the view expressed by Galloway and Goodwin (1987) that:

> The most effective procedures for preventing rather than treating, disturbing or maladjusted behaviour are a by-product of processes,which aim to raise the overall quality of education for pupils in the school.

However, beyond such important general issues of approach and attitude, there are certain specific areas of school organisation, which have particular relevance to 'keeping clever' those pupils who might otherwise become disaffected. First, as the Elton Report acknowledges, it is necessary to recognise that the quality of the content of the curriculum and the teaching and learning methods through which it is delivered are important influences on pupil behaviour (DES, 1989: para. 4, p.71). Second, in meeting the demands of mixed ability teaching required to avoid rigid streaming arrangements which reject low achievers from the mainstream of school life, it is useful to consider whether the concept of support teaching, a system devised for helping pupils with learning difficulties, might be extended to develop a comprehensive yet flexible system of support for helping teachers deal with pupils whose behaviour causes problems for discipline in schools.

CURRICULUM DEVELOPMENT

Strong concerns were expressed to the Elton Enquiry that the introduction of the National Curriculum, with its prescribed programmes of study and established attainment targets stating what children should be expected to know and do at certain ages, might make school life more difficult for less able and low achieving pupils and thereby lead to more disruption (DES, 1989: para. 4, pp. 69–70). It was argued that pupils who experience failure in academic subjects may see school as boring and irrelevant and it is members of this group who are most likely to behave badly. Taking the full range of subjects required by the National Curriculum might squeeze out of the timetable some of the more adventurous alternative curricular offerings, often with a clearly highlighted 'vocational' element which are designed to appeal to low achieving fourth- and fifth-year secondary pupils.

Since the Education Act 1981 abolished the traditional terminology of categories of handicap, it has been the practice to discuss provision for pupils with special educational needs in terms of whether they require a 'modified' or a 'developmental' curriculum or whether their curricular needs can be met in the 'mainstream with support'. Wherever possible, it is the latter which has been seen as the preferred option. Whilst it is not difficult to see how modifications can be made to take account of physical or sensory impairments without any derogatory implications, it may well be that for youngsters with difficulties in learning an 'alternative' or 'modified' curriculum can easily be seen as a confirmation that they have been academically written off by the school. For these and other low achievers their entitlement to follow the National Curriculum may reduce their sense of rejection by the system.

Much will depend on how successfully courses are developed which are lively, stimulating and matched to the abilities and interests of pupils with a wide range of abilities. This is not an easy task and the Elton Report identifies various aspects of school organisation, curriculum development and delivery which require special consideration. For example, whilst an emphasis on academic achievement is a good thing in itself, if this is the only source of success and esteem within a school, it may lead to problems with low-achieving pupils. Similarly, rigid streaming by ability has an effect on pupils' self-respect and the Elton Report urges schools to examine carefully their policies on setting, banding and other means of grouping by ability to avoid generating feelings of rejection and hostility. Inefficient teaching fails to match learning tasks to pupils' abilities and thereby leads to yet more boredom, frustration and a potential source of trouble in the classroom.

The apparent lack of relevance of many learning experiences particularly for older pupils is another factor which may explain a lack of co-operation from less able pupils who do not see the purpose or point for them of some parts of the curriculum. There is a cultural insensitivity in some schools to their pupils' social and ethnic backgrounds and often a failure to make the most of opportunities to affect attitudes and behaviour through the curriculum for moral, personal and social education. Developing a sense of the school as a community which appreciates and values all its members is a matter of planning appropriate learning experiences as much as a statement of educational philosophy.

CLASSROOM MANAGEMENT

Although these aspects of curriculum planning will require decisions in policy making at senior management level, there are also many ways in which the individual classroom teacher can help avoid disaffection by helping maintain the motivation and interest of low-achieving pupils at a more personal and individual level. Indeed meeting special educational needs can be said to begin when effective classroom management prevents a minor problem with learning or behaviour from becoming a more severe or complex difficulty. By analysing their own methods of lesson organisation and delivery, teachers can often identify situations which raise or lower a child's self-esteem.

In reflecting on their own experience teachers may find it helpful to think in terms of what have been described as the 'four rules' of classroom management: get them in; get them out; get on with it; and get on with them (Laslett and Smith, 1984; Smith, 1989). Effective teachers 'get them in' by starting lessons smoothly and promptly, not only getting pupils physically into their places on time but also mentally tuning them in to the lesson itself. Providing short, simple tasks which recapitulate the previous lesson or give a reminder of the skills needed for the next activity offers a reassurance that new learning will be within the pupil's competence. Occupying the class in this way also gives the teacher time to deal with registration or other administrative duties and to cope more easily with the petty irritations of lost or malfunctioning equipment. Too dilatory a beginning to a session can lead to a reluctance to start work at all; too demanding an opening to a lesson can lead to a feeling that as the topic is well beyond the learner it is hardly worth trying.

The ending of the lesson is another time when the pupil's feelings of competence and confidence can be enhanced or diminished. Teachers who 'get them out' effectively, give thought to the orderly routine with which they conclude their work, collect materials and put books away but they also make sure that every opportunity is taken to refresh, restate and reinforce the theme of the lesson. Sometimes a game or quiz or song or story can end a session on a suitably lighter note leaving even the less successful student with the feeling that whilst never going to be a favourite activity even a difficult subject can offer some pleasure.

The pupil's sense of competence and self-esteem in a particular subject area depends to a great extent on how successfully teachers manage to 'get on with it', in the sense that they maintain the momentum of lessons by selecting suitable content and ensuring that it is delivered with appropriate variety and pace. Nothing succeeds like success but nothing frustrates more than failure and failure leads almost inevitably to disaffection. Many problems in management would be avoided if there were more careful scrutiny by individual teachers and by subject departments of the suitability of textbooks and learning activities for mixed ability teaching. Too often work is set for a notional mid-ability range which leaves the most able unstretched and the least able untouched. At either end of the spectrum of ability, attention should to be given to providing alternative and supplementary materials. Where there are specific difficulties in reading and writing, help can be given through providing topic summaries and study guides which identify and explain key words and concepts. Alternative methods of response, such as tabulating information, labelling and subdividing texts offers a change from traditional essay or comprehension exercises. Working in pairs or small groups can be a valuable experience of co-operative learning as well as providing support for pupils whose ability might otherwise be underestimated because of literacy problems.

Working with groups rather than dealing only with the class as a whole, helps with the fourth rule of classroom management: 'get on with them'. Teachers build good personal relationships with children through becoming more aware of them as individuals. The strengths and weaknesses of some pupils who can easily fade into anonymity as part of a class of thirty are much more visible when they are being dealt with as part of a group of five or six. Becoming sensitised to individual characteristics will make it easier to tailor tasks to ability and to ensure that every pupil is able to achieve that sense of progress and accomplishment which is essential to encouraging continued effort where natural talent is lacking.

Working with groups will involve considerable planning of physical arrangements as well as personal approach. Classroom layout or design may need rethinking to take account of changed patterns of traffic control and increased movement. It might be useful to set up 'learning centres' or 'resource islands' so that groups can work in turn on particular aspects of a topic. This approach is also especially suitable for team teaching which can allow one member of the team to concentrate on looking after the needs of pupils with difficulties in learning.

SUPPORT

The traditional view of remedial teaching as an activity for which a pupil is withdrawn from the mainstream for special tuition and coaching has been supplanted in recent years by the concept of 'support teaching'. Intervention takes the form of supporting colleagues with ideas, methods and techniques as much if not more than with direct teaching. Traditional aspects of remedial work such as diagnostic advice on specific learning difficulties and the adaptation of material to provide suitable learning activities are still part of the service but increasingly the support teacher is seen as someone whose job involves developing a whole school approach to meeting the special needs of children with learning difficulties.

This idea is very much in tune with the Elton Report's encouragement for the development of whole-school behaviour policies backed up by local authority support systems drawing on educational psychologists and educational welfare officers as well as talented teachers. It is useful, therefore, to reflect on what can be learned from the progress so far of the concept of special needs support in producing whole-school policies.

Discussing integration at the time when the 1981 Act was about to be implemented, Potts (1983) argued that meeting special needs in the ordinary school should involve 'examining curricula, groupings, time-tabling, teaching styles and the present use of existing people, buildings and equipment'. Instead of being the consequence of such a radical reappraisal of school organisation the support teacher has come to be looked upon as the catalyst for change. Rather than being a means towards helping achieve carefully planned and financed policies for integrated education, the provision of support teaching seems to have become an end in itself. The mere presence of a support teacher in some schools appears to be sufficient to satisfy the feeling that something is being done about special needs, although the organisational arrangements for fulfilling the role may be insufficient to ensure that its effect is more than marginal. Similarly the statement of a behaviour policy or the appointment of a member of staff as 'facilitator' for in-service training or 'mentor' for new teachers, may be no more than a token response to the Elton Report unless accompanied by an appropriate allocation of resources.

Dyer (1988) comments that support must be prevented from becoming 'a humpty-dumpty word meaning whatever anyone chooses to make it mean'. This can be avoided if the three applications or 'strands of support', which Dyer describes, are interwoven so that support is provided for pupils through individual attention, for teachers through collaborative teaching and for schools through advice on curriculum planning and delivery. It is this last strand which can most easily become unravelled, at least in part because there is confusion and tension between the roles of consultant and co-operative teacher. It is not easy to combine the status of the authoritative expert with that of the facilitative assistant. Being perceived as a supporter in the classroom may not encourage acceptance at the level of being an agent of change for the school as a system.

If the concept of support teaching is taken as an example of what has happened to one initiative for introducing a whole-school policy, it does raise certain questions about what will happen if a similar approach is to be considered for implementing a whole-school policy for behaviour and discipline. Do support teachers get much say in what is going on or is their job seen as merely tempering the wind to the shorn lamb with special needs? Are support teachers seen as inspirational advisers to the teacher or nursemaids to the pupil? Are they treated as curriculum consultants or classroom au-pairs? Are they regarded as academic co-pilots or educational baggage handlers? These issues of status are important if changes in policy and practice are to be implemented.

When the idea of the whole-school approach was first introduced in Scotland in response to an HMI report recommending a new approach to teaching pupils with difficulties in learning, it was launched as an official regional policy with the full backing of the education authority and the allocation of special resources. It involved the early appointment of principal teachers to prepare for the new initiative, the organisation of area teams linking work in primary and secondary schools and the appointment to each team of experienced teachers who were required to undertake additional training. In comparison, attempts to introduce a similar system in England appear piecemeal and haphazard.

Without a concerted and properly funded policy initiative, the response in England to the notion of widening responsibility for meeting special needs has depended to a major extent on individual goodwill and mutual understanding between support teachers and the class teachers with whom they work. Though there are many examples of individual good practice, there is no clear national policy and even within individual local education authorities there is wide divergence in provision between schools. There are already signs that the eminently sensible suggestions and recommendations of the Elton Report will produce a similar patchwork of response dependent on individual initiative and enthusiasm.

At least a national priority for training in classroom management has been identified and money has been earmarked for providing it. However, there are no precise indications of how that money should be spent or exactly what should be involved in the training. It is to be hoped that such training will look at difficulties in learning and behaviour together, examining curriculum and teaching methods to see where frustrations arise and preventing them from becoming sources of friction. Discipline in schools is not simply a matter of making pupils conform to a prescribed code of conduct. It is about providing and maintaining an environment conducive to enabling pupils to fulfil their academic potential or, as Hargreaves' informant put it more colloquially, it is about 'keeping them clever'.

REFERENCES

DES (1989) *Discipline in Schools (The Elton Report)*, London: HMSO.

Dyer, C. (1988) 'Which support?' *Support for Learning* 3: 6–11.

Evans, M. (1981) *Disruptive Pupils*, London: Schools Council.

Galloway, D. and Goodwin, C. (1987) *The Education of Disturbing Children*, London: Longman.

Hargreaves, D. (1967) *Social Relations in a Secondary School*, London: Routledge & Kegan Paul.

Laslett, R.B. and Smith, C.J. (1984) *Effective Classroom Management: a teacher's guide*, London: Croom Helm.

Mortimore, P., Sammons, P., Stoll, L., Lewis, D. and Ecob, R. (1988) *School Matters: the junior years*, London: Open Books.

Potts, P. (1983) 'Summary and prospect', in T. Booth and P. Potts (eds) *Integrating Special Education*, Oxford: Basil Blackwell.

Rutter, M., Maughan, B., Mortimer, P. and Ouston, J. (1979) *Fifteen Thousand Hours: secondary schools and their effects on pupils*, London: Open Books.

Smith, C.J. (1989) 'Weathering classroom disruption', *Special Children* 26: 7–9.

5 Whole-school approaches to disruption: What part can psychology play?

Robert Burden

It is of some significance that whilst the Elton Report is entitled *Discipline in Schools* (DES, 1989), in many people's minds the Enquiry upon which the Report is based was mainly concerned with disruptive behaviour. It is quite understandable that the two are often seen as synonymous, but one of the strengths of the Elton Report is that it tries very hard not to fall into that particular trap. Thus, in many respects it is concerned with ways of *preventing* disruptive behaviour and sees positive discipline very much in this light. In doing so, it follows the lead of a far less vaunted (but in its own small way equally impressive) document, *Education Observed 5, Good Behaviour and Discipline in Schools* (DES, 1987).

At the risk of labouring the point, it is perhaps worth noting that the two Reports had rather different starting points. We are told (DES, 1989) that the Elton Enquiry was established 'in response to concern about the problems facing the teaching profession' (p.11) and that 'we were particularly concerned by reports that physical attacks by pupils on members of staff were commonplace and the cause of widespread anxiety among teachers', (p.8) even though it found no evidence for the latter. *Education Observed 5*, on the other hand, started with the premise that 'good behaviour is a necessary condition for effective teaching and learning to take place' (p.1) and drew its conclusions from a number of specific visits to schools where high standards of behaviour were known to exist. In the end, both Reports reached the same conclusion, that the behaviour of pupils in a school is influenced by almost every aspect of the way in which it is run and how it relates to the community it serves.

The trouble with the Elton Report is that it is essentially a responsive pragmatic document. The same is true, to a somewhat lesser extent, of *Education Observed 5*. Both documents take as their premise that learning can only take place in situations where 'good' behaviour (nowhere defined) is the norm and where it is the duty of those in power (teachers) to control those who are there to learn. It is not that bad behaviour is seen as mainly the fault of the pupils, but it is taken for granted, for example, that 'rewards' and 'punishments' are natural and necessary features of schools and that the dispensation of these in a fair and rational manner will help to establish a 'good' learning environment. No account is taken here of the distinction drawn by the philosopher P.S. Wilson (1971) between *control* and *discipline*.

> 'control' is a way of ordering things which is considered necessary for getting something done. By contrast, a 'discipline' is the form of logical and evaluative order which must be learned if one is to understand what is involved *in doing* something.
>
> (Wilson, 1971, p.77)

Thus, if children are made to behave in certain ways, however positive that behaviour may be, as a result only of externally imposed rewards or sanctions without fully understanding the reasons for the required behaviour, let alone entering an agreement to behave in a particular way as a result of gaining that understanding, they can be said to be subject to control but not to discipline. Moreover, there is a strong case to be made that true 'self-discipline' can only arise out of an understanding of the nature of the 'social contract', never from the bland atmosphere of even the most positive forms of school organisation.

The Elton Report only really gets to grips with this issue at one point (para. 31, p.66) where it refers to the purposes of the school curriculum as defined by the 1988 Education Reform Act as promoting 'the spiritual, moral, cultural, mental and physical development of pupils and preparing them for the opportunities, responsibilities and experiences of adult life.' However, whilst emphasising the importance of this broad view of curriculum and acknowledging that schools exist to teach values as well as knowledge and skills, the members of the Elton Committee appear not to be aware of the essential mismatch of many of their recommendations with these avowed aims.

As one whose personal definition of applied psychology involves helping people to understand why they behave in the way that they do and encouraging them to predict the probable consequences of one way of behaving as compared with perceived alternatives, it strikes me that the Elton Committee might have benefitted from a more psychological approach involving some degree of conceptual analysis. Of course, this is not a view shared by the Elton Committee who seem to see educational psychologists as having two main functions. The first is to act as swiftly as possible, i.e. within six months, to get 'truly' disruptive pupils 'statemented' under the terms of the 1981 Education Act. The second, more promising, view (para. 18 p.184) is that educational psychologists should play a much wider role in promoting good behaviour in schools and that 'LEAs should encourage closer working relationships between schools and educational psychologists to develop consultancy services providing advice on the management of behaviour in groups and in the schools as a whole.' However, this laudable aim falls into the trap of failing to define the term 'consultancy', whilst the use of the associated term 'advice' implies a particularly narrow conceptualisation.

The role of the educational psychologist as consultant is one which I have explored at length in several articles (Burden, 1980, 1981) and which I have had the opportunity of developing by means of a 'spiral consultancy' with educational psychology colleagues working for Somerset and Devon LEAs (Brown and Burden, 1987; Nichols *et al.* 1989). With the members of the Devon Psychological Service in particular, I have been able to approach the issue of preventing disruptive behaviour in a series of school-focused projects (Nichols and Burden, 1989).

The Devon Psychological Service is not alone in wanting to move in the direction of providing consultancy service to schools, nor is it necessarily any more advanced than any other Services in the United Kingdom (Mercer *et al.*, 1990) or the USA (Gutkin and Curtis, 1981). However, there are undoubtedly certain unique aspects about how its 'whole-school approach' developed and is currently being applied which seem worth recounting. As Plas (1986) has stated, there are still too few accounts of the process of applying systems psychology to schools in comparison with speculative theoretical treatises on how it might be done.

In South Devon two key variables were the existence of close links between the educational psychologists and the author, who was known to be keen on fostering the consultancy role (both for himself and others) and the presence of a visiting research fellow from Western Australia, who had pioneered something similar in his own home territory (Hamilton, 1987).

Following a highly successful one-day awareness course entitled 'Combating disruptive behaviour', to which a number of secondary schools had indicated their willingness to become actively involved in a different way or working with their educational psychologists, it was decided to set aside a regular time-slot for the South Devon team and the two consultants to meet regularly with this aim in mind. This resulted in one half-day meeting per fortnight throughout one school term. A possible working format for a whole-school approach to managing student behaviour was provided by Hamilton (1987) and the psychologists' team discussed ways in which this might be implemented in secondary schools in their area using a teamwork approach. The author's role at this stage was to serve largely as a process consultant.

The basic format of the Western Australian approach was for the consultant to negotiate with an interested secondary school the setting up of a team of between ten and twelve people, including the headteacher and at least one basic grade teacher, who were to work together under the consultant's guidance for a minimum of two hours per week over ten weeks. Each of these sessions was centred upon a specific aspect of managing student behaviour in the following order.

1 A framework for considering resistant students based on the assumptions that every teacher has a right to teach and every student has a right to learn.
2 Analysing disruptive incidents, with particular reference to the ideas of Rudolf Dreikurs.
3 The importance of teachers taking a positive approach in the classroom.
4 Essential communication skills: active listening.
5 Essential communication skills: sending clear messages.
6 An example of a whole-school approach to discipline: William Glasser's Reality Therapy (Glasser, 1969).
7 Setting clear limits in the classroom: rules.
8 Setting clear limits in the classroom: sanctions.
9 Conflict resolution – a general problem-solving approach.
10 Putting it together in the school: developing strategies for implementation at the whole-school level.

At the end of these sessions the 'discipline team' was expected to continue working together on a regular basis until they had formulated a discipline plan to present to the rest of the school staff for discussion and, ultimately, for implementation.

Using this kind of framework, it is possible to specify programme objectives with regard to pupils, teachers and the school. Thus, it is to be expected that:

1 Pupils
   • will engage in less disruptive behaviour in the classroom and around the school
   • will indicate that within the school their needs are acknowledged.
2 Teachers
   • will demonstrate an awareness of a range of skills for effectively managing pupil behaviour
   • will integrate these skills into their on-going teaching practice
   • will experience a reduced level of stress in their interaction with pupils

3 The school
  - will review its current approach to discipline and will produce a written discipline policy
  - will develop a set of procedures to operationalise that policy
  - will implement that policy
  - will acknowledge the importance of continual professional discussion for effective behavioural management and therefore facilitate regular teacher interaction to this effect
  - will regularly review and evaluate its new discipline policy in direct relationship to the pastoral needs of its pupils.

It can readily be seen how the content of this course is in accord with both the spirit and many of the recommendations of Elton. It can also be seen how it differs from both this and other approaches such as BATPACK (Wheldall and Merrett, 1985) PAD (Chisholm *et al.*, 1986) and the in-service courses provided by Leeds (Mercer *et al.*, 1990) and other LEA psychological services. First, the course is eclectic in drawing upon a number of theoretically sound psychological approaches to behaviour management, ranging from positive teaching to counselling skills and reality therapy. Second, it begins with the assumption that whilst many of the problems faced by teachers are very similar, no two schools are the same; it is, therefore, school-focused. Third, it assumes that working alone even the most charismatic leader will have enormous difficulty in bringing about change – thus the need for a 'discipline team' representing a critical mass of the school staff. Fourth, the role of the outside consultant is emphasised as a key figure in modelling, encouraging, team building, training and providing process feedback to the participants. In this respect the approach is very akin to aspects of organisational development (Fullan *et al.*, 1980).

As a result of the South Devon team discussions a number of steps were taken to fit the Western Australian approach to the British context. For example, it was felt necessary to offer a certain degree of flexibility with regard to the number of staff involved in the discipline team and the time and siting of meetings. As the psychologists also saw the need to develop their own teamwork, they decided to work in pairs. On one occasion when *all* of the staff at one school indicated their willingness to become involved (i.e. forty-eight teachers), three psychologists and three trainees from Exeter University's professional training course in educational psychology ran the programme together. Since the availability of good supply teachers and the money to pay them was at a premium, sessions tended to take place after school and on school premises. This is not ideal. At least one part of the success of the Western Australian experience is perceived by Hamilton as having been related to the fact that the teachers were freed to work at the issues in school time, in comfortable surroundings, away from the school premises.

A policy document arising out of the psychological service team's discussions was sent to all secondary schools in the South Devon area. (An approach to dealing with behaviour problems in primary schools was also developed concurrently, but will not be described here.) This document emphasised the team's desire to offer schools a service which was:

1 preventative as well as supportive;
2 continuous rather than intermittent;
3 available to as many staff as possible;
4 of value to the whole school;
5 focused on positive development rather than negative behaviour; and
6 provided by a team rather than merely by individual psychologists.

It also spelled out a number of steps to be taken if a school wanted to negotiate further action along these lines (see Nichols *et al.* 1989 for a reproduction of this document).

The response from schools was immediate, mainly positive and potentially overwhelming. Fortunately, partly as a consequence of supportive funding from Exeter University, it proved possible to build in on-going evaluation of courses provided to several schools (Williams, 1988; Gil, 1990). A number of internal documents were also produced on the process of consultancy and training during each of the sessions on one of the courses. All of these documents are of an 'illuminative' nature (Parlett and Hamilton, 1977) and reflect to some extent the growing interest at Exeter in so-called 'new-paradigm' research methodology (Reason and Rowan, 1981) and action research (McNiff, 1988).

In the spirit of such enquiry, evaluation outcomes were not assessed in terms of test results or statistical data. What did become evident, however, was an enhanced degree of teacher commitment and feelings of empowerment (Williams, 1988) and changes in one school's discipline structure by involving all school participants (including pupils, secretaries and dinner ladies) (Gil, 1990). The latter study and an internal, unpublished study of another project were also helpful in highlighting key factors associated with the perceived success of such ventures. The size and constitution of the 'discipline team' is clearly important, as also is the way in which that team decides to 'spread the word' to other members of staff in order to guarantee that commitment and involvement in any changes that take place. The attitude of the headteacher plays an important part, especially with regard to such issues as the release of personal power. We have also found that different schools are at different stages of readiness for change and that some have first to work through their own hidden agenda before they are able to take on real curriculum change and development of the kind described here.

This latter point raises two further issues, namely the skills of the consultant and the importance of process over content. A fundamental mistake of otherwise useful curriculum packages such as PAD is the assumption that any interested group of teachers can take it off the shelf and simply apply the ideas contained within the manual and videotape for their own and their colleagues' benefit. Nothing could be further from the truth. Access to a well-trained and sensitive external consultant will almost always be necessary to help any large secondary school system to 'shift' in the desired direction. This is not to say that the consultant need always play the leading role, although, as outlined earlier he or she may make a considerable input of content. What the consultant *must* do, however, is to identify at an early stage the readiness of the school to change and any potential blockages to such change, whilst acting throughout as a catalyst and facilitator. Williams (1988) provides an in-depth description of such a consultant in action and, in doing so, helps to identify some of the key skills involved. It has long been the aim of the Exeter University Educational Psychology Training Course to prepare its trainees to begin to undertake such a role (Burden, 1980).

The increasing emphasis on the notion of 'process-based courses' is hopefully well illustrated in the following example of a one-day course run by two educational psychologists with the whole staff (forty-two teachers) at a secondary school in response to a request from the school to help them look at their discipline policy. The consultants were not known to the school, nor had they any knowledge of it apart from the fact that it was a medium-sized, single sex, secondary school with a reputation for being 'tough'. The brief they had been given by the first deputy, who had arranged the day, led the consultants to believe that an illuminative, action research approach would ultimately be of greater benefit to the school than one which concentrated upon attempting to impart skills of behaviour management.

A structure for the day was therefore devised which incorporated individual reflection, working in pairs and small groups, sharing in larger groups and by means of posters summarising each group's conclusions and, finally, by large group discussion. Having negotiated with the staff how they wished to work, the consultants then provided the following tasks:

1   an exploration of the term 'disruption' and a comparison of disruptive with disturbed, delinquent and maladjusted behaviour;
2   a specification of the kind of behaviour most commonly epitomising disruption throughout the school day, where and when it most

commonly occurred and what were the most common antecedents and consequences;

3 the need to specify what would commonly represent positive behaviour;

4 a sharing of the kinds of things that happened in classes and around the school to (a) encourage positive behaviour and (b) foster negative behaviour;

5 brainstorming ways of increasing and improving 4(a) whilst decreasing and eliminating 4(b)

6 a discussion of different kinds of explanations as to why children misbehave and the implications of such implicit theories for individual and systematic action;

7 reactions to a video presentation of William Glasser's whole-school approach to discipline;

8 a whole-group discussion of what would be involved in producing a whole-school discipline policy and how it would differ from what was currently taking place.

The aim of the consultants throughout the day was to get the staff of the school to 'own' the problems with which they were faced and to recognise that most of the solutions lay in their own hands. Reactions at the end of the day made it clear that this had been largely achieved but that there were huge obstacles to change within the management hierarchy of the school and in what was essentially a 'split' staffroom over teaching styles and learning outcomes. These were problems which, it was clear to all, had to be tackled before any effective pastoral or curriculum change could be brought about.

SOME TENTATIVE CONCLUSIONS

The main underlying theme of this chapter is that the Elton Report is an interesting and positive document, but it does not go nearly far enough. Pragmatic approaches to fostering 'good' behaviour in schools are of limited value if they are not contextualised within a coherent theory of teaching and learning. If teachers do not function, in Donald Schoen's words (Schoen, 1983), as 'reflective practitioners', they will never understand the differences between discipline and control. Whole-school discipline policies developed without such reflection may well help to keep disruptive behaviour to a minimum in the short term, but are unlikely to foster a shared community feeling or generate responsible, socially oriented thinkers and actors.

Psychology in its broadest sense and educational psychologists in particular have a great deal to offer here; the former by providing a means of gaining greater understanding of why people behave in the way that they do, the latter by taking on the vitally important role of process consultant. The challenge to the discipline and to the practitioners is a clear one.

REFERENCES

Brown, E. and Burden, R.L. (1987) 'Educational psychologists as agents of School Organistional Development: consultants or reformers?', *Educational Change and Development* 8: 19–21.

Burden, R.L. (1980) 'Educational psychologists as school-based consultants: the Totnes project', in E.C. Raybould, B. Roberts and K. Wedell (eds) *Helping the Low Achiever in the Secondary School*, Birmingham: Educational Review.

—— (1981) 'The educational psychologist as instigator and agent of change in schools: some guidelines for successful practice', in I. McPherson and A. Sutton (eds) *Reconstructing Psychological Practice*, London: Croom Helm.

Chisholm, B., Kearney, D., Knight, G., Little, H., Morris, S. and Tweddle, D. (1986) *Preventative Approaches to Disruption*, Basingstoke: Macmillan.

DES (1987) *Education Observed 5, Good Behaviour and Discipline in Schools*, London: HMSO.

—— (1989) *Discipline in Schools (The Elton Report)*, London: HMSO.

Fullan, M., Miles, M.B. and Taylor, G. (1980) 'Organisational development in schools: the state of the art', *Review of Educational Research* 50: 121–83.

Gil, M. (1990) 'An evaluation of a whole school approach to managing pupil behaviour, unpublished M.Ed. (Ed.Psych.) dissertation, University of Exeter.

Glasser, W. (1969) *Schools Without Failure*, New York: Harper & Row.

Gutkin, T.B. and Curtis, M.J. (1981) 'School-based consultation: the indirect service delivery concept', in C.R. Reynolds and T.B. Gutkin (eds) *The Handbook of School Psychology*, New York: Wiley.

Hamilton, P. (1987) 'An evaluation of a school discipline programme – "Managing Student Behaviour: a whole school approach"', unpublished M.Sc. thesis, Murdoch University, Western Australia.

McNiff, J. (1988) *Action Research: principles and practice*, London: Macmillan.

Mercer, S., Costa, P. and Galvin, P. (1990) 'Making discipline positive and making it work!', *Educational Psychology in Practice* 5: 210–15.

Nichols, S.L. and Burden, R.L. (1989) 'Developing a consultancy approach within a Psychological Service', *Educational Psychology in Practice* 6, (in press).

Nichols, S.L., Parffrey, V. and Burden, R.L. (1989) 'Preventing disruptive behaviour in schools: the educational psychologist as school system consultant', *School Psychology International* 10: 265–73.

Parlett, M. and Hamilton, E. (eds) (1977) *Beyond the Numbers Game*, London: Macmillan.

Plas, J. (1986) *Systems Psychology in the Schools*, Oxford: Pergamon Press.

Reason, P. and Rowan, J. (1981) *Human Inquiry*, Chichester: Wiley.

Schoen, D. (1983) *The Reflective Practitioner: helping professionals think in action*, London: Temple Smith.

Wheldall, K. and Merrett, F. (1985) *The Behavioural Approach to Teaching Package*, Birmingham: Positive Products.

Williams, S.A. (1988) 'A whole school approach to managing pupil behaviour: an evaluation, unpublished M.Ed. (Ed.Psych.) dissertation, University of Exeter.

Wilson, P.S. (1971) *Interest and Discipline in Education*, London: Routledge & Kegan Paul.

6 Effective classroom behaviour management: Positive teaching

Kevin Wheldall and Frank Merrett

Effective classroom behaviour management is an essential prerequisite for effective classroom learning. It is a necessary, but not, of course, a sufficient condition for learning to take place. If the teacher is prevented from teaching, or pupils are prevented from getting on with their academic work as a result of their own inappropriate or disruptive classroom behaviour, or that of others, then clearly little learning of value can take place. The child whose behaviour is continually disruptive, or who is even quietly but regularly off-task, is seriously educationally disadvantaged, since we know that academic engaged time is one of the most important correlates of academic progress.

Problems of discipline and classroom control have been perennial concerns for teachers but, until recent years, academic educationists and teacher trainers have largely ignored these issues focusing instead on such matters as curriculum design and content. Little or no specific training in managing classroom behaviour has typically been provided for teachers at either pre- or in-service level, as the Elton Report makes clear (DES, 1989). Our own findings from a recent study (see Chapter 2) confirm that the vast majority of teachers claim to have learned to manage classes 'on the job', by trial and error, with little or no training in behaviour management having been provided in their teacher training courses.

THE POSITIVE TEACHING PROJECT

The origins of what was to become the 'Positive Teaching Project' may be traced to the mid-1970s when we began carrying out preliminary studies on troublesome classroom behaviour. In 1981 we were awarded a research project grant from the now defunct Schools Council to develop our methods into a training course for teachers. Originally known as the Behavioural Approach To Teaching Project, we began to produce prototype versions of the first of our Positive Teaching Packages for use as an in-service course in general classroom behaviour management in primary schools.

Our project had four major aims and areas of study:

1 to determine the nature and extent of classroom behaviour problems faced by teachers;
2 to determine how teachers typically respond to pupils' classroom behaviour;
3 to devise and evaluate experimentally (positive) methods for increasing appropriate classroom behaviour and decreasing inappropriate behaviour;
4 to develop and evaluate experimentally courses for training teachers in effective classroom behaviour management.

Before considering these research areas in more detail, it is appropriate at this point to spell out what we mean by 'positive teaching' and how it relates to the Behavioural Interactionist Perspective (BIP).

POSITIVE TEACHING AND THE BEHAVIOURAL INTERACTIONIST PERSPECTIVE

Our research is predicated on a conceptual model of positive teaching (Wheldall and Merrett, 1984; 1989; Merrett and Wheldall, 1990a) based on applied behaviour analysis and observed classroom processes. In essence the procedures we advocate 'accentuate the positive' by requiring teachers to focus their attention on pupils when they are behaving appropriately ('catch them being good') rather than continually being on the lookout for, and reprimanding, inappropriate behaviour. We suggest a number of procedures which have been shown experimentally to bring about improved classroom behaviour, often requiring teachers to change their own teaching behaviour or to make changes in the classroom environment. When presenting our methods to teachers on our Positive Teaching Package course, we boil down the underlying model to five key principles and concentrate on skills training, rather than labouring under a weight of theory. The five principles of positive teaching are:

1 Teaching is concerned with the observable.
2 Almost all classroom behaviour is learned.
3 Learning involves change in behaviour.
4 Behaviour changes as a result of its consequences.
5 Behaviours are also influenced by classroom contexts.

These principles are fairly straightforward and we will not dwell on them here. They are detailed in the books referred to earlier.

The procedures we advocate have all been rigorously evaluated and have been shown repeatedly to be very effective. Our research and positive teaching procedures are characterised by a concern with ecological classroom variables and setting events for classroom behaviour, as well as contingency management procedures. They are also child centred in the sense that pupil initiations and negotiations constitute critical components of BIP (Wheldall and Glynn, 1988; 1989). Our research, then, is not only conceptually coherent but has also attempted to advance a new, more contemporary behavioural model of teaching and learning. The ten characteristics of the BIP are as follows:

1   Adheres to the methodology of applied behaviour analysis.
2   Recognises the importance of naturalistic antecedent events.
3   Strives to maximise the use of naturally occurring reinforcers.
4   Responds to empirical evidence from non-behavioural theoretical perspectives.
5   Emphasises the mutuality and reciprocity of behaviour in teacher/ learner interactions.
6   Seeks to assist children to assume a greater degree of control over their own learning.
7   Focuses on broader educational issues than just schooling.
8   Encourages initiations by the learner.
9   Values the learning opportunities provided by errors.
10 Recognises the complex professional skills required of teachers.

Again, we will not dwell here on these characteristics of BIP, except to comment that the perspective is behavioural in that it builds on the methods and principles of behaviour analysis but is equally interactionist, since it is based on the central idea that we all (teachers and pupils) learn from each other by interacting with each other. As will be readily apparent, there are several major points of departure from the traditional (we would say 'dated') behavioural position. This contemporary behavioural perspective rejects the notion of totally teacher-directed, tightly sequenced, errorless learning programmes built on behavioural objectives and monitored by endless behaviour checklists and favours, instead, behavioural operationalisations of more naturally occurring learning experiences which capitalise on child initiations, on naturally occurring antecedents and consequences and on the contribution all tutors (teachers, parents, peers) can make to effective teaching. We believe this perspective to be more ecologically valid since, by being based more on natural learning experiences, resulting learning/changes in behaviour are more likely to be maintained and to generalise to other contexts. These points are elaborated in the sources referred to earlier by Wheldall and Glynn. We will now proceed to attempt to demonstrate the application of these principles in the context of effective classroom behaviour management. First, however, it is important to clarify just what classroom behaviours teachers regard as particularly troublesome. This was the first of our four aims of the Positive Teaching Project.

CLASSROOM BEHAVIOUR PROBLEMS

Disruptive behaviour in the classroom is widely acknowledged as being one of the major problems facing many, if not most, teachers, and children with behaviour problems are a common type of referral to educational psychologists. Before we completed our studies, however, there was some confusion as to the exact nature of the problem. It was widely believed by the media and some sections of the community that classroom violence and serious disorder and disruption were rife in schools. We carried out surveys in both primary and secondary schools which enquired into the frequency and kinds of troublesome behaviour experienced by teachers in their class-rooms, in order to attempt to determine the nature and extent of the problem.

The primary survey (Wheldall and Merrett, 1988) constituted a 25 per cent random sample (thirty-two schools) of the infant, junior and junior/ infant schools in a West Midlands education authority. Replies were received from all thirty-two schools resulting in a very high return rate of 93 per cent, with 198 teachers responding.

Half of the sample (51 per cent) responded affirmatively to our first question, 'Do you think that you spend more time on problems of order and control than you ought?' with the same percentage of men and women responding in this way. The average class size was twenty-seven of which 4.3 children, on average, were regarded by their teachers as troublesome. Three of these were boys. Asked to identify the two most troublesome individual children in their class, 76 per cent of the teachers identified boys as the most troublesome and 77 per cent of the teachers identified boys as the second most troublesome. This supports the anecdotal view that boys do tend to be regarded as more troublesome than girls.

What was it that these children did that was so troublesome? It was the type and frequency of troublesome behaviours in which we were parti-cularly interested. We offered ten alternative behaviour categories based on information from our pilot enquiries. When asked to pick out the most troublesome behaviour, 46 per cent of teachers cited 'talking out of turn' (TOOT), which was defined as calling out to the teacher when not called upon, chattering about non-work related matters, and making unwanted comments and remarks. This was followed by 'hindering other children' (HOC), chosen by 25 per cent of teachers. None of the other categories was chosen by more than 10 per cent of teachers. The findings for the most *frequent* troublesome behaviours gave a very similar picture and when we went on to ask about the troublesome behaviours of individual children cited as being troublesome, again we got the same pattern of responses, TOOT followed by HOC. The category 'physical aggression' was cited by fewer than 1 per cent as being most troublesome and this placed the category tenth (last) in rank order.

We subsequently carried out a survey of the opinions of secondary school teachers in the West Midlands (Houghton *et al.* 1988b) using a very similar questionnaire. The survey was based upon a random sample (about 30 per cent) of the secondary schools in the same West Midlands district as before. Replies were received from all six schools approached yielding a return of 62 per cent. Of the 251 secondary teachers responding, 55 per cent admitted to spending more time on problems of order and control than they ought. Once again TOOT (50 per cent) and HOC (17 per cent) were readily identified as by far the most frequent and troublesome classroom mis-behaviours. Physical violence and verbal abuse were, again, very rarely cited. As at the primary level, boys were identified as the most troublesome pupils by the majority of teachers. These findings at the secondary level are particularly interesting as it is often claimed that the problems facing secondary teachers are different from, and more serious than, those facing primary teachers.

But it appears safe to assume that the classroom behaviour problems experienced by most primary and secondary school teachers are similar. TOOT and HOC appear to be the two misbehaviours which teachers generally identify as causing them the most trouble and as occurring most often. This is not to say that serious incidents do not occur occasionally in some schools but they are certainly not as frequent as the media would have us believe. Physical violence appears to be a problem encountered (thank-fully) by relatively few teachers, but many, if not most, teachers have their job made more difficult by the frequent occurrence of the petty mis-behaviours which we have identified.

We believe that we were at least among the first to show that the major behaviour problems facing both primary and secondary school teachers were relatively minor misbehaviours which occurred with very high fre-quency. The media and teacher unions were united in citing classroom violence as being the major concern but the Elton Report (DES, 1989) confirms, by independent research inspired by the evidence we formally presented to the Committee of Enquiry, that what we refer to as 'talking out of turn' is by far the most pressing discipline problem facing teachers.

Most teachers would agree that TOOT and HOC are not particularly serious misbehaviours, in the sense that they are hardly crimes; but they are irritating, time-wasting, exhausting and stressful. The good news is that these sorts of classroom problem behaviour have been shown to be particularly amenable to resolution by positive teaching methods at both primary and secondary levels. Before considering examples of positive teaching procedures in action, we will first consider how teachers typically respond to pupils in terms of their use of approval and disapproval, praise and reprimand; the second of the four aims of the Positive Teaching Project.

TEACHER RESPONSES TO CLASSROOM BEHAVIOUR

Positive teaching advocates increasing teacher praise and approval and decreasing disapproval and reprimands. But a typical response from teachers to the suggestion that they should be more positive in their interactions with children and to use praise more freely is to claim, 'Ah, but we do that already'. And, to a certain extent, this is true. The procedures advocated are indeed very similar, if not identical, to the procedures utilised by many skilled teachers; nor is this surprising since few children would learn very much that is useful and desirable if these principles were not sometimes being followed. But relatively little is known about the ways in which teacher approval and disapproval are normally employed in classrooms. Consequently, we carried out large-scale observational studies of British primary- and secondary-school teachers to determine 'natural rates' of teacher approval and disapproval.

Brophy (1981) has made the point that praise may or may not function as a positive reinforcer and that teachers may employ praise for purposes other than reinforcement. This may well be true but we know that praise can function as a reinforcer when used in a careful and systematic way. When observing teacher behaviour in the classroom, however, it is very difficult to tell whether praise delivered is reinforcing or not, in any objective way. What we can do is to sample overall use of praise (and disapproval) and to bear these reservations in mind when we consider our results.

As part of the Positive Teaching Project, we carried out two large-scale observational studies of primary- and secondary-school teachers and their classes. Merrett and Wheldall (1987) report findings based on a sample of 128 British primary- (and middle-) school teachers and Wheldall *et al.*, (1988) provide parallel results from a sample of 130 secondary-school teachers. In both studies, the OPTIC (Observing Pupils and Teachers in Classrooms) schedule, was employed, a schedule we developed as part of this research programme. We were interested to know in how much of the lesson observed children in the class spent working and in the nature and frequency of teachers' responses to their behaviour. OPTIC allows the observer to sample systematically positive and negative teacher responses to children's academic work and social behaviour and also children's on-task behaviour. Studies carried out by our students working in pairs have shown the schedule to be both reliable and valid. A full account of OPTIC and its development is to be found in Merrett and Wheldall (1986). In our studies, each teacher and class were observed on three separate occasions for half an hour each time.

Analyses of the primary-school data revealed total rates of approval (56 per cent) as higher than total disapproval (44 per cent), with more teacher responses given to academic work (66 per cent) than to classroom social behaviours (34 per cent). In terms of academic behaviours alone, positive teacher responses occurred three times more frequently than negative responses, whereas for social behaviours alone, negative responses were five times more frequent as positive responses. Of the 128 teachers observed, thirty-eight of them *never* expressed any approval towards social behaviour, whilst six of them each gave over twenty such responses, clearly reflecting the variability between teachers. The pupils in the classes observed were found to be on-task for an average of 70 per cent of the time.

The subsequent study involving secondary-school teachers and their classes, to our surprise, revealed a very similar pattern of responding. Overall approval (55 per cent) was again higher than overall disapproval (45 per cent) and more comments were made in response to academic behaviours (59 per cent) than to social behaviours (41 per cent). For academic behaviours alone, positive responses were three times as frequent as negative responses, but for social behaviours negative responses were three times as frequent as positive responses. Considerable variability was evident in teacher behaviours; for example, approval to social behaviour was never expressed by twenty-six of the 130 teachers, whilst seven of them each gave over twenty such responses. The mean percentage on-task behaviour of the classes observed was about 80 per cent which suggests, in so far as this sample is representative, that British secondary-school pupils spend a very high percentage of their time engaged in activities defined as appropriate by their teachers.

British teachers, then, in general, *approve* slightly more than they *disapprove*. In fact, approval for academic behaviour is much higher than disapproval. But for social behaviour the reverse is the case. Teachers are very quick to notice social behaviour of which they disapprove and continually nag children about it. But they hardly ever approve of desirable social behaviour. In other words, children are expected to behave well without the need for praise and are continually reprimanded if they do not. In positive teaching we encourage teachers to use *at least* twice, and preferably three or four times, as many praise statements as reprimands.

This brings us, logically, to the third of our aims: to devise and evaluate experimentally positive methods for increasing appropriate classroom behaviour and decreasing inappropriate behaviour. Positive teaching methods may be roughly divided into the use of antecedents and the use of consequences, although many methods involve the use of both, as we shall see. Let us first consider the use of antecedents.

USING ANTECEDENTS TO INFLUENCE CLASSROOM BEHAVIOUR

In the literature reporting behaviour analytic studies of classroom behaviour management, the vast majority of studies reported are based on contingency management procedures in which the consequences of classroom behaviour are systematically manipulated. Far fewer studies emphasise the role that antecedents can play in effective classroom behaviour management. And yet procedures based on the careful manipulation of antecedents can have many advantages, as we have argued elsewhere (Wheldall, 1982; 1988; Wheldall and Glynn, 1988, 1989). Such procedures often require less effort from teachers, are less complicated, are less artificial and yet can lead to equally impressive gains in appropriate behaviour which may be more easily maintained and which show greater ease of generalisation to other settings. We will not dwell on these points here but instead present two examples of effective use of antecedent control.

Let us first consider classroom seating arrangements, an area of particular interest in which we have carried out a series of studies. Since the practice was strongly commended in the Plowden Report, children in most primary classes in this country sit around tables in groups of four, five or six. The justification for this was that children can learn from each other through discussion and co-operation. However, for this to stand any chance of success, the nature of the work set must be a group activity requiring collaboration. The reality is that whilst seating may have changed, the work demands have not. Much of the work set is still individually based, children being expected to work on their own, using work cards, for example. As a consequence, much of the talk in table groups tends to be chatter not related to the work in hand. There is mis-match between the nature of the tasks and the seating arrangements leading to less time spent on-task and less work being completed.

We carried out parallel studies in two junior schools with classes of 10 to 11 year old children (Wheldall, Morris, Vaughan and Ng, 1981). One class consisted of twenty-eight boys and girls of mixed ability attending a school in an urban residential area, whereas the other consisted of twenty-five similar children from a school on a council housing estate. In both classes, the children normally sat around tables in groups. The children in both classes were initially observed for two weeks (ten days) in their normal seating arrangements around tables. An obser- vation schedule was employed to obtain estimates of on-task behaviour. This was defined as doing what the teacher had asked, i.e. pupils looking at and listening to her when she was talking to them, looking at their books or work cards when they were required to complete set work, only being out of their seats with the teacher's permission and so on.

After observing the class for two weeks sitting around tables the desks/ tables were moved into rows without comment from the teacher, and the children were observed for a further two weeks using the same procedure. Finally, the desks were moved back to their original positions, again without comment, for a further two weeks of observation. This time there were complaints from the children as some of them said they preferred sitting in rows.

In both classes on-task behaviour rose by around 15 per cent overall when the children were placed in rows and fell by nearly as much when they returned to sitting around tables. Looking at individual children, the most marked improvements (over 30 per cent) occurred for those whose on-task behaviour had previously been very low. As we might expect, the effect was less in the case of those with high initial on-task behaviour.

Subsequent studies have replicated these findings many times and have also shown that on-task behaviour remains high even after several weeks of sitting in rows. Moreover, we have shown that the quantity and the quality of work produced is greater when children are seated in rows. Let us emphasise immediately, however, that we are not advocating a back to rows movement for all children for all work. What we are saying is that teachers should vary the seating arrangements to suit the task in hand.

Most of us would advocate that, ideally, children should be given as much choice as possible as to where they sit and with whom. In classrooms arranged in table groups this almost inevitably results in girls and boys being seated around separate tables. Similarly, in classes where children sit in rows, children of the same sex prefer to sit next to each other. Teachers sometimes claim, however, that one of the most effective ways of curbing the disruptive behaviour of children, particularly boys, is to sit them next to a member of the opposite sex. The aim of the following study was to determine whether mixed-sex seating does, in fact, produce such clear effects, in terms of changes in on-task behaviour (Wheldall and Olds, 1987).

The study was carried out with two classes in a junior school in an inner-city area. One class consisted of 31 mixed ability children (16 boys,

15 girls) aged 9 to 10 years and the other comprised 25 similar 10 to 11 year old children (13 boys and 12 girls). Both class teachers were female. In the younger class, the children were seated at six groups of tables. Three of the groups of tables were occupied solely by girls, the other three by boys. During the intervention phase of the study, the boys and girls were mixed so that boys and girls were now sitting next to each other. In the other class, the children were seated at conventional double desks, not tables. The desks were arranged in three rows and all of the children usually sat next to a member of the opposite sex. During the intervention period, girls and boys in each row changed places so that they were now sitting by a member of the same sex.

Again, in this study the two classes were first observed for two weeks in their usual seating conditions followed by a two-week intervention phase. Observations carried out under the changed seating conditions were then followed by two more weeks of observation with children back in their usual seats. The results clearly showed that on-task behaviour in the older class, seated in rows, decreased (by 15 per cent) when the children of the same sex sat together. In the younger class, seated in groups, on-task behaviour increased (by about 15 per cent) when the normal same-sex seating was changed in favour of mixed-sex seating. The conclusion to be drawn is that mixed-sex seating produces the highest pupil on-task levels. Similarly, disruptive behaviour in both classes was at its lowest when boys and girls sat together. What also emerged clearly from the results was that children with the lowest on-task study levels were most positively affected by the change from mixed to same-sex seating.

We are not necessarily advocating any particular type of seating arrangement, although there are some occasions when control of seating can be used to good effect; to establish some measure of control with an unruly class, for example. What we would emphasise, once again, is the importance of flexibility; of matching the seating arrangements to the task in hand. More generally, positive teachers seek to optimise the classroom environment so as to encourage appropriate behaviour and effective learning.

The ways in which the curriculum is delivered can also be important functional antecedents for classroom behaviour. Quiet reading periods are a case in point. A widely agreed goal of primary education is to foster in pupils an affinity for books and reading. Consequently, once some of the basic skills of reading have been mastered, many teachers timetable quiet reading periods for their pupils, often on a daily basis, in an attempt to encourage reading for its own sake. Meanwhile, teachers often busy themselves by engaging in classroom chores such as pinning up work, marking books, writing on the blackboard or, more commonly, by hearing individual children read aloud. This can be distracting for the silent readers and may also become a cue for children to chat among themselves instead of reading. Quiet reading is thus not perceived to be an important or worthwhile activity.

Teachers can demonstrate the importance of reading as a recreational activity by modelling the desired behaviour of quiet reading. This is sometimes referred to as Uninterrupted Sustained Silent Reading (USSR). We recently carried out several studies demonstrating that teacher modelling of appropriate reading behaviour during USSR sessions consistently leads to marked increases in the amount of time pupils spend actually reading (Wheldall and Entwistle, 1988).

These studies were again carried out in two primary schools with third- and fourth-year junior classes. In all four classes silent reading sessions were held frequently but the teachers typically used these times to listen to individual readers or to carry out other tasks in the classroom. During these experiments, at the start of all sessions, the teachers announced clearly that it was to be a quiet reading time and the children were to read their own books. Whilst USSR was in operation and the teachers were modelling reading, the children were informed that it was to be a quiet reading time, that the teacher had his or her own book to read which was very interesting and did not want to be disturbed. The teacher then sat reading the book in a prominent position. Observation sessions lasted for the first fifteen minutes of each daily session of fifteen to twenty minutes duration and the amount of time the children spend reading quietly was recorded.

The first study, which lasted six weeks, involved a class of 23 10 to 11 year olds. During the initial sessions, time spent reading averaged 50 per cent but this figure rose to a mean of 73 per cent during the first USSR phase when the teacher modelled silent reading. This level dropped back to 56 per cent when USSR was discontinued and rose again to 82 per cent when it was reintroduced. In other words, USSR led to around 25 per cent increases in time spent reading. In a second, bigger study with three third- and fourth-year classes, the results were equally clear. In all three classes, the amount of time spent actually reading during USSR sessions was, on average, between 20 per cent and 30 per cent higher than usual. We also looked at the number of individual pupils whose behaviour was influenced by teacher modelling of silent reading. Further data were collected from ten individual children and we found that eight of them had clearly increased the amount of time they spent quietly reading during USSR sessions.

This series of studies demonstrates the effectiveness of USSR in encouraging quiet recreational reading and, more generally, how teacher behaviour is an important antecedent for pupil behaviour. The teachers involved in these studies said that their pupils were now reading more books than they usually did. This was partly a result of them having more regular reading sessions but also because they spent more time actually reading during the USSR sessions. The ways in which we deliver the curriculum are clearly important functional antecedents for behaviour as these studies show.

THE USE OF NATURAL CONSEQUENCES

A key feature of positive teaching, deriving from the BIP, is its emphasis on naturally occurring consequences. As we have argued elsewhere (Wheldall, 1982), the use of heavy, unnecessarily intrusive reinforcers can be counterproductive, leading to problems of maintenance and generalisation to other settings. We have termed this 'behavioural overkill' in the context of advocating an increased role for antecedents, as described above. To illustrate the use of positive teaching involving naturally occurring consequences, we have chosen two non-intrusive interventions; one from early years teaching and one from teaching high-school students.

The use of touch by teachers is an under-researched area, in spite of the prevalence of use of this form of non-verbal communication, especially by teachers involved in early childhood education. We have carried out both observational studies exploring the functions of touch and its distribution and, more importantly, experimental studies assessing its potential for use as a classroom reinforcer (Wheldall *et al.*, 1986).

The aim of these experimental studies was to determine the effect of positive contingent teacher touch on the classroom behaviour of infant-class children. We wanted to know whether reducing the use of non-contingent touch and increasing the use of positive contingent touch to accompany praise by teachers, would lead to children's on-task behaviour increasing and their disruptive behaviour decreasing. Our first behavioural intervention was carried out with two infant classes and their teachers in a small primary school.

Each teacher and her class were observed for ten half-hour sessions, using an early version of the OPTIC schedule (described earlier) adapted to include teacher touch behaviour. Following the baseline sessions, both teachers were instructed to touch children only when they praised them for appropriate academic and/or social behaviour and not to touch children for other purposes. It was emphasised that no deliberate increase of praise was required or to be attempted. Both teachers were again observed, as before, for a further ten sessions. In both classes when teachers touched children together with praising them, on-task behaviour rose by over 15 per cent, from around 75 per cent to 90 per cent, and disruptions fell from about ten or eleven per session to only two or three instances. Both teachers substantially increased their contingent use of touch (mainly linked to approval for academic behaviour) and decreased their use of non-contingent touch.

The second intervention study was carried out to replicate the first but using a more rigorous, multiple baseline design with two further infants classes. The procedure was introduced into the second class a week after being introduced into the first class. Data on on-task behaviour and teacher behaviours were collected for fifteen minutes each day, for three weeks. Baseline data collection began on the same day for both classes but whereas this consisted of only one week (five sessions) in class 1 prior to intervention, in class 2 the baseline condition was extended to two weeks (ten sessions) prior to intervention. Data collection continued for a further two weeks following intervention in class 1 and a further one week in class 2, according to the multiple baseline design. For both classes the intervention consisted of instructing the teachers to touch the children only when they were praising them and not to attempt to increase the rate of praise. For class 1 on-task behaviour rose from nearly 40 per cent to nearly 70 per cent and for class 2 from 50 per cent to 65 per cent, when teacher touch was paired with praise. Both teachers were successful in reducing their overall use of non-contingent touch, following the interventioń, and increased their contingent use of touch (i.e. accompanying approval) substantially.

These two studies, involving four teachers, provide evidence for the effectiveness of teacher touch as a reinforcer for appropriate classroom behaviour, when accompanying praise. In all four cases mean class on-task behaviour increased substantially following the inclusion of touch, by an average of 20 per cent and, where measured, rates of disruptive behaviour fell markedly. In other words, across the four different studies, children spent about one-third as much time again working compared with baseline levels. Given four replications of the effect, this is reasonably strong evidence for the effectiveness of teacher touch combined with praise as a natural but powerful reinforcer of young children's classroom behaviour. Moreover, interventions like these based on naturally occurring reinforcers are also more likely to lead to the learned behaviours generalising to other settings.

Positive teaching, clearly, tends to be associated with strategies based on praise and reward. Teacher nagging for inappropriate behaviour has been shown to be ineffective and is not recommended although, as we have shown earlier, it is commonly and frequently employed by teachers. But this is not to say that there is no place for the occasional use of discreet reprimands, as another study, we carried out with research students showed (Houghton *et al.*, 1990). We compared two behaviour management procedures in four high-school classes, using a multiple baseline design. Two of the four teachers taking part in the study were found to use high rates of loud reprimand and low use of praise with their classes. Following baseline observations, these two teachers were asked to limit their use of reprimands to ten or fewer, per lesson. They were also asked to move closer to the pupil when reprimanding, to make eye-contact and to state quietly but firmly exactly what was being disapproved of. In both classes on-task behaviour increased by around 15 per cent and rose a further 10 per cent when a second strategy, private, specific praising, was also introduced.

The other two teachers, who used few reprimands and few praise statements during baseline, were initially asked to give twenty private, specific praise statements per lesson. On-task behaviour rose by about 12 per cent as a result and increased by a further 6 or 7 per cent when the two teachers were also asked to employ up to five private reprimands per lesson. Taken together, the results for the four teachers suggest that there is a role for reprimands if used sparingly, specifically and privately and in a positive context overall. Private reprimands are less likely to lead to confrontations as the pupil reprimanded is less likely to lose face with his or her peers. There is also evidence to suggest that older, high-school pupils respond better to more private forms of praise. Survey data, based on high-school pupils' attitudes to various forms of praise, reward, reprimand and punishment supports these experimental findings (Houghton *et al.*, 1988a).

In the above studies, we have sought to demonstrate how naturally occurring consequences such as touch, praise and reprimands can be effectively employed in behavioural interventions to bring about increased levels of appropriate classroom behaviour. To avoid 'behavioural overkill', one should employ only the lightest interventional strategy necessary to bring about the desired effect, employing manipulated antecedents and naturally occurring reinforcers. But there will, of course, be times when a slightly more intrusive strategy may be justified, perhaps with pupils evidencing more troublesome behaviour. In such cases, we should continue to bear in mind another central tenet of the BIP, that we should seek to assist pupils to assume greater control over their own learning and to foster independence. Just one example will demonstrate such an approach in action, combining the use of antecedents and consequences.

Pupils themselves can be directly involved in bringing about behaviour change. Older primary- and high-school pupils, for example can be encouraged to monitor their own behaviour and to determine whether they are on- or off-task, as the following studies illustrate (Wheldall and Panagopolou-Stamatelatou, 1991). The first study involved a junior class of thirty pupils aged between 9 and 10 years. Preliminary observations were made of the class using the OPTIC observation schedule. After data had been collected for six sessions over a period of two weeks the teacher showed her class a graph of the preliminary data so that they could see 'how hard they were working'. This graphical representation of their (low) on-task behaviour, surprised them. They agreed that they would like to do something about it and so the self-recording procedure was introduced.

Every child was provided with a simple recording sheet for each session. For thirty minutes, during the lesson, a tape was played which emitted an audible signal at irregular intervals, but on average once per minute. The children were instructed to record their behaviour, as either on- or off-task, on the self-recording sheet every time that the signal was heard.

To enable children to decide whether or not they were on-task, the teacher negotiated a set of positive rules with them. These rules were: we remain in our seats when we do boardwork, we put up our hands when we want help and we can only come out to get equipment during the investigation task. The teacher reminded children of them before each lesson. Children who had been on-task were awarded three housepoints at the end of the lesson.

In the final phase of the study three further observation sessions were completed during one week without self-recording. The teacher alone carried out the observations and at the end she showed the children the graph of their on-task behaviour (which had increased) and praised them. She then invited them to try to maintain their high on-task rate without listening to the signal and recording themselves.

On-task behaviour during the preliminary observations averaged only 64 per cent but increased markedly to 96 per cent when self-recording was introduced. When self-recording was discontinued the average on-task level fell back to 85 per cent. These results indicate a clear, immediate and enduring effect for self-recording. An interesting side-effect of this study was that negative teacher responses also declined appreciably during self-recording since there was so little inappropriate behaviour to criticise.

During the final phase the level of on-task behaviour fell, providing evidence for the effectiveness of the strategy, but remained relatively high, providing some evidence for maintenance and generalisation. This may have been partly due to the set of rules used as a frame of reference for the children, which had allowed them to decide whether, or not, they were on-task and which were still in force.

Consequently, we carried out a second study to attempt to replicate these findings without employing rules. Three mixed-ability primary classes in the same school took part in an across classes, multiple baseline design study in which self-recording was introduced to the three classes at staggered intervals. In addition to the class as a whole, three target individuals from each class were observed individually. These target children were selected by their teachers because they were perceived as wasting a lot of time in off-task behaviours. Once again, all three classes were observed using the OPTIC schedule. Preliminary observations were carried out for differing numbers of sessions for each class before the self-recording strategy was introduced. Again the teachers showed the children a graphical representation of their own on-task behaviour and discussed with them the importance of being on-task.

Self-recording contributed to an increase in average on-task behaviour for all classes: from 72 per cent to 83 per cent in the first class; from 64 per cent to 93 per cent in the second class and from 65 per cent to 87 per cent in the third class. Further, follow-up observations of the third class when self-recording was discontinued showed a subsequent decrease in on-task behaviour to 69 per cent. Of the nine individual target children observed, eight showed evidence for clear gains in average on-task behaviour as a result of self-recording. The amount of work produced by the three target children in the third class was also examined. The average number of words written in half an hour during preliminary observations was eighty-one but rose to 127 during self-recording and then fell back to ninety-nine words during follow-up observations.

Self-recording strategies, and all of the other methods and procedures which were shown experimentally to be effective, are included in our Positive Teaching Packages for training teachers in effective classroom behaviour management. This brings us to the fourth and final aim of the Positive Teaching Project, the development and evaluation of effective teacher training courses in positive teaching.

TRAINING TEACHERS IN THE SKILLS OF POSITIVE TEACHING

Having determined the nature of the behaviour problems facing teachers, and examined how teachers typically respond to such behaviour, we became involved in devising training courses for teachers which draw on our programme of research and which teach the various skills and procedures we have demonstrated (experimentally) to be effective. The skills-based training packages we have developed are based firmly on our conceptually coherent model of positive teaching. Hence the training packages are not merely atheoretical collections of 'tips for teachers' but offer a generative model for effective classroom teaching. The model consists of a theoretical framework for understanding classroom behaviour in terms of teacher–pupil interactions, a methodology for analysing classroom behaviour problems and a technology for solving them.

The first training package to be developed was the Behavioural Approach to Teaching Package (BATPACK), (Wheldall and Merrett, 1985), for use in primary schools, which was published in 1985. In 1988 we published our secondary package – the Behavioural Approach to Teaching Secondary Aged Children (BATSAC), (Merrett and Wheldall, 1988). Our aim was to change teacher behaviour by means of skills-based training carried out on site with the staff of a school. These courses comprised six one-hour units held weekly after school. Teachers contract to attend all sessions on time and to attempt to implement the various skills and strategies taught during the session in their classrooms during the following week. For example, teachers monitor their frequency of use of praise and reprimands using a tally counter to increase their awareness of their performance and, if necessary, to change it.

The courses have consistently yielded very positive evaluations from teachers attending them but we have adopted a very stringent approach to their dissemination. Not only have we demanded that all tutors must be trained to tutor the packages but we have also been prepared to release the packages for use by other tutors *only* when the packages were clearly and consistently shown to be yielding major, measurable changes in both teacher and pupil behaviours. Our programme of research and development has been characterised by continual, rigorous, objective evaluation of successive versions of the training packages based on direct observation of teachers and classes before and after training. This is rare in British educational research.

Independent evaluations of courses not taught by us have confirmed our findings that following course attendance, teachers appreciably decrease their use of reprimands, increase their use of praise and reward and, most importantly, bring about substantial positive changes in the behaviour of their classes. Average on-task levels in schools have been shown to rise by 10 to 20 per cent with some individual classes gaining appreciably more. This means that, on average and depending on the initial levels of on-task behaviour, pupils may be spending up to a third more time actually working than previously. Subsequent studies have shown that these increases in time spent working are accompanied by increased work output.

These findings of increased productivity have been confirmed, for example, in a larger-scale study involving the whole staff of a large primary school who received BATPACK training in two groups (Merrett and Wheldall, 1990b). Of the twenty-three teachers attending the courses, twenty-two completed our pre- and post-training questionnaires. Nine agreed to be observed before and after BATPACK training and twelve teachers agreed to collect samples of their pupils' written work before and after they (the teachers) had taken the course.

The twenty-two teachers demonstrated a clear positive shift in attitude towards positive teaching methods after taking the course and all of them said that they would recommend BATPACK training to a colleague. Almost all thought that they had increased their use of positive responses and most thought that they had decreased their use of negatives. Similarly, the group as a whole were far more likely to select solutions based on positive teaching approaches to solving classroom behaviour problems after the course than before.

Once again, classroom observations showed that the nine teachers observed had increased their overall rates of positive responding on average by 60 per cent and had reduced their negative responding to only 30 per cent of pre-course levels. Except for one class, where the pupil on-task level was already in excess of 90 per cent, all classes increased their levels of on-task behaviour, by an average of over 13 per cent, from just over 68 per cent to nearly 82 per cent. Finally, the amount of written work produced by pupils increased significantly after teachers had completed the course. Prior to the courses, pupils averaged fifty-eight written words per fifteen minutes but afterwards this rose to seventy-three, an increase of over 25 per cent. Thus, we have increasing evidence that BATPACK training successfully changes teacher behaviour which, in turn, influences children's behaviour. Following our training courses the amount of time pupils spend on-task increases substantially and this is accompanied by increased work output.

There are now about a thousand trained and registered tutors qualified to teach our training courses, not only in the UK but also in Australia, New Zealand, Hong Kong and Canada. Reports of its effectiveness in practice have continued. Recently, we have been developing the package further. The new Positive Teaching Packages (primary and secondary), to be released in 1991, are extensively revised five-unit versions of our earlier packages. The results of a recent study in which seven teachers were observed before and after training with this new version have been most encouraging. Not only were the teachers very enthusiastic but their behaviour had changed markedly. Their use of positives increased substantially, so that they were subsequently using twenty times as many positives to social behaviour as before. Negatives fell to half their original levels. Every class improved on their pre-training level of on-task behaviour as a result of the course, increases ranging from 6 to 20 per cent and averaging 13 per cent.

The significance of our work in this area is perhaps best demonstrated by reference yet again to the Elton Report. Not only are our findings corroborated by the research carried out for the Report but the Report also specifically recommends our training package as an in-service training resource in classroom management. More generally, we have demonstrated that change can effectively be brought about in schools by positive means. We have demonstrated that teachers can do something constructive about troublesome classroom behaviour rather than blaming parents, television or food additives. Positive teaching focuses on encouraging pupils to learn to behave more appropriately and hence to stand more chance of learning effectively in school. It offers hope to teachers and educationists that schools can become less alienating, aversive and unresponsive and more positive, liberating and effective.

REFERENCES

Brophy, J. (1981) 'Teacher praise: a functional analysis', *Review of Educational Research* 51: 5–32.

DES (1989) *Discipline in Schools (The Elton Report)*, London: HMSO.

Houghton, S., Merrett, F. and Wheldall, K. (1988a) 'The attitudes of British secondary school pupils to praise, rewards, punishments and reprimands: a further study', *New Zealand Journal of Educational Studies* 23: 203–14.

Houghton, S., Wheldall, K. and Merrett, F. (1988b) 'Classroom behaviour problems which secondary school teachers say they find most troublesome', *British Educational Research Journal*, 14: 295–310.

Houghton, S., Wheldall, K., Jukes, R. and Sharpe, P. (1990) 'Are reprimands really necessary? The effects of limited private reprimands and increased private praise on classroom behaviour in four British secondary school classes', *British Journal of Educational Psychology* 60: 255–65.

Merrett, F. and Wheldall, K. (1986) 'Observing pupils and teachers in classrooms (OPTIC): a behavioural observation schedule for use in schools', *Educational Psychology* 6: 57–70.

—— (1987) 'Natural rates of teacher approval and disapproval in British primary and middle school classrooms, *British Journal of Educational Psychology* 57: 95–103.

—— (1988) *The Behavioural Approach to Teaching with Secondary Aged Children (BATSAC) Training Package*, Birmingham: Positive Products.

—— (1990a) *Positive Teaching in the Primary School*, London: Paul Chapman.

—— (1990b) 'Does training of teachers in behavioural methods result in higher pupil productivity?', *Educational and Child Psychology* 7: 31–43.

Wheldall, K. (1982) 'Behavioural pedagogy or behavioural overkill?', *Educational Psychology* 2: 181–4.

—— (1988) 'The forgotten A in behaviour analysis: the importance of ecological variables in classroom management with particular reference to seating arrangements', in A. Feiler and G. Thomas (eds) *Planning for Special Needs: a whole school approach*, London: Basil Blackwell.

Wheldall, K., Bevan, K. and Shortall, K. (1986) 'A touch of reinforcement: the effects of contingent teacher touch on the classroom behaviour of young children', *Educational Review* 38: 207–16.

Wheldall, K. and Entwistle, J. (1988) 'Back in the USSR: the effect of teacher modelling of silent reading on pupils' reading behaviour in the primary school classroom', *Educational Psychology* 8: 51–66.

Wheldall, K. and Glynn, T. (1988) Contingencies in contexts: a behavioural interactionist perspective in educated', *Educational Psychology* 8: 5–19.

—— (1989) *Effective Classroom Learning: a behavioural interactionist approach to teaching*, London: Basil Blackwell.

Wheldall, K., Houghton, S. and Merrett, F. (1988) 'Natural rates of teacher approval and disapproval in British secondary school classrooms', *British Journal of Educational Psychology* 59: 38–48.

Wheldall, K. and Merrett, F. (1984) *Positive Teaching: the behavioural approach*, London: Allen & Unwin.

—— (1985) *The Behavioural Approach to Teaching Package For Use in Primary and Middle Schools (BATPACK)*, Birmingham: Positive Products.

—— (1988) 'Which classroom behaviours do primary school teachers say they find most troublesome?', *Educational Review* 40: 13–27.

—— (1989) *Positive Teaching in the Secondary School*, London: Paul Chapman.

Wheldall, K., Merrett, F. and Borg, M. (1985) 'The Behavioural Approach to Teaching Package (BATPACK): an experimental evaluation', *British Journal of Educational Psychology* 55: 65–75.

Wheldall, K. and Olds, D. (1987) 'Of sex and seating: the effects of mixed and same-sex seating arrangements in junior classrooms', *New Zealand Journal of Educational Studies* 22: 71–85.

Wheldall, K. and Panagopoulou-Stamatelatou, A. (1991) 'The effects of pupil self-recording of on-task behaviour on primary school children', *British Educational Research Journal* 17: 113–27.

Wheldall, K., Morris, M., Vaughan, P. and Ng, Y.Y. (1981) 'Rows versus tables: an example of the use of behavioural ecology in two classes of eleven year old children', *Educational Psychology* 1: 171–84.

7 An ecosystemic approach to classroom behaviour problems

Paul Cooper and Graham Upton

In this chapter we propose an ecosystemic approach to classroom behaviour problems and attempt to identify the potential value of such an approach to teachers and schools. We suggest that our proposed ecosystemic approach:

1 offers new ways of conceptualising behaviour problems in schools, which are based on the view that human behaviour is developed and maintained through interactional processes;
2 offers teachers a new range of strategies for dealing with emotional and behavioural problems, which emphasise collaborative approaches to problem solving and the central importance of individuals' phenomenological interpretations in the development of solutions (though not, necessarily, the phenomenological interpretations of all involved individuals);
3 offers specific and practical measures which may lead to the enhancement of the overall effectiveness of schools, stressing as they do the power that is derived from the appreciation of differing, sometimes conflicting personal perspectives on situations and the importance of giving consideration to human individuality. This approach not only offers assistance to pupils and their teachers but also has important implications for relationships among staff and between staff and parents.

It is important to stress from the outset that we are not proposing any kind of simplistic analogy between the classroom and the family. Our approach draws on family therapy sources, but is informed by a specifically educational perspective, which emphasises the distinctive qualities of the school/classroom situation and the existing specialised skills of teachers. We must also emphasise that we do not suggest that practising teachers can or should develop the level of skill and expertise possessed by trained family therapists. We are suggesting, however, that it might be possible for teachers to make profitable use of systemic insights, and particular intervention techniques which follow from these insights, in their everyday interactions with students, students' parents/families and colleagues.

Our major concern is to place the ecosystemic approach within the humanistic tradition of British education which emphasises the need for schools to be run on democratic, person-centred lines, with their ultimate goal being the development of autonomous, self-directing individuals. We argue that teachers, and consequently schools, in order to be 'effective', must give prominence to humanistic principles in their daily practice (Cooper, 1989). Our approach can also be seen in the context of the current concern for increased school effectiveness, as exemplified in the Elton Report (DES, 1989), and in the increasingly important role of teachers as guardians of children's rights, as a consequence of the 1989 Children Act (Bridge and Luke, 1989).

THE ORIGINS OF THE ECOSYSTEMIC APPROACH

Systemic Theory and Recursive Causality

From an ecosystemic viewpoint, human behaviour is the product of on-going interaction between environmental influences and internal motivations which derive from prior (mainly social) experience. Furthermore, the overarching, twin human needs for a recognised personal identity and a sense of social belonging, make the social group (or 'system') the central focus of human activity, to the extent that individuals' personal needs and motivations are often subordinate to those of the group as a whole. The potential for conflict, both interpersonal and intra-personal, in such circumstances is obvious. All group members depend upon the group to supply particular needs, thus the maintenance of the group is paramount, even if its maintenance requires the sacrifice of one of its members.

The theoretical origins of this view of human behaviour rests in the work of Ludwig von Bertalanffy (1950; 1968) and Gregory Bateson (1972; 1979), and in the clinical practice of pioneer family therapists, such as Selvini-Palazzoli (Selvini-Palazzoli *et al.*, 1973), Minuchin (1974), and de Shazer (1982; 1985). Von Bertalanffy is responsible for the original formulation of 'General System Theory' (von Bertalanffy, 1950; 1968). This theory argues that the physical and social sciences can be seen to share a common concern with analysing data in systemic terms. A key tenet of General System Theory is that simplistic notions of causation are inadequate, and that living organisms share the characteristic of purposiveness, by which they act upon stimuli rather than simply responding to stimuli in a unilinear manner. Thus, causation is seen in terms of circular configurations (referred to by Bateson [1979] as 'recursive'), characterised by the cybernetic concept of 'feedback', whereby the goals of the system (including the maintenance of the system itself) are achieved through resisting stimuli which are not directed toward the system's goals (negative feedback), and through promoting and encouraging stimuli which serve the system's goals (positive feedback). The inter-connectedness of elements within a system also means that change in any part of the system will reverberate throughout the system. Family therapy techniques are based on these principles.

Family Therapy

Our perspective draws on three major approaches to family therapy (Speed, 1984), each of which emphasises particular elements in the ecosystem of family dysfunction (that is, a particular range of influences on interactional events). These approaches are not mutually exclusive and are often combined by therapists. The aim of therapy is always to promote positive change in the family system which enables the family to function effectively and without the need for the destructive interactional patterns that have grown up around the symptomatic individual. Each therapeutic model offers a systemic analysis of interpersonal interaction in families and together they provide us with a range of analytical tools for developing systemic analyses of classrooms and other interactional systems.

For our purposes there are a number of principles under which the various approaches to family therapy unite:

1   the aim of therapy is to promote positive change in situations characterised by interactional patterns (i.e. patterns of feedback and reinforcement, by which particular behaviours are perpetuated or suppressed) which are harmful to one or more of the family members;
2   this makes the interactional system the focus for intervention, rather than any individual member, since it is the system which functions to maintain the undesired situation;
3   successful change depends upon the quality of 'fit' between the chosen intervention and the existing pattern of family functioning (i.e. the intervention must be an alternative pattern of behaviour which is perceived by the family or family sub-system as viable);
4   accurate knowledge of the pattern of family functioning is only achieved by a therapist who is willing and able to form a co-operative relationship with family members, and is, in effect, able to 'join' with the family to create a therapeutic system which facilitates the exposure of the interactional patterns surrounding problem behaviour and the perceptions and personal meanings underlying them;

5 the need for the therapist to control personal bias and to achieve both a detached and deepened understanding of the family situation is facilitated by the use of a therapeutic team, whose presence is often hidden behind a two-way mirror during therapy sessions, results in the generation of additional and often divergent perceptions of what they observe. This 'poly-ocular view' (de Shazer, 1985) promotes creativity which is necessary for the generation of appropriate interventions;

6 once an appropriate intervention is put into action, the feedback mechanisms in the family system take over, and thus a new interactional pattern is established. The therapist is no longer required, having facilitated a positive solution which utilizes the family's inherent capacity for self regulation.

The Term 'Ecosystemic'

We choose the term ecosystemic (after de Shazer, 1982; Molnar and Lindquist, 1989) with extreme care. The most common use of the word 'ecosystem' is as a term to describe the interdependence of living things in the natural world. The chief characteristic of an 'ecological' perspective is a concern for the way in which small changes in any part of the ecosystem have consequences which are amplified throughout the global environment. This concept of interdependence and recursive causation is central to the approach to human interaction described here, which stresses the ways in which human systems constantly adapt in order to minimise the destructive effects of change and in so doing create new patterns of interaction.

This is a different view from that associated with the term 'systems approach', as proposed by social theorists such as Parsons (1951). Such theorists espouse a mechanistic view, seeing human behaviour as being constrained by the social system, to the extent that action by the individual is seen to be ineffectual. From such a viewpoint, systems change is only achieved through the exercise of power by groups of individuals or by individuals with a disproportionate share of power.

AN ECOSYSTEMIC APPROACH TO SCHOOL BEHAVIOUR PROBLEMS

A significant proportion of the work of family therapists is concerned with childhood behaviour problems. It is not surprising, therefore, that in recent years many family therapists (particularly in America) have begun to focus some of their attention on the school system as a factor in family difficulties which manifest themselves in childhood behaviour problems. Lindquist *et al.*, (1987) suggest that school-related problems are best characterised in one of three ways, as (a) a problem in the family that disturbs the school, (b) a problem at school that disturbs the family, or (c) a problem at school that does not disturb the family. Smith (1978), Worden (1981) and Okun (1984) all describe ways in which students' problem behaviour in school can sometimes be related to difficulties in the family system.

In Britain, Dowling and Osborne (1985) have developed what they describe as a 'joint-systems' approach to a wider consideration of the school ecosystem, seeing the school as an important influence on the pupils' behaviour. They, therefore, advocate that family therapists act as consultants to the school system as well as the family system, as appropriate. Taylor and Dowling (1986) and Dowling and Taylor (1989) describe the setting up of an outreach service, whereby a group of family therapists make themselves available, on a regular basis, to parents and teachers by basing themselves on school premises. Campion (1985) also advocates the training of British educational psychologists in family therapy techniques, as a means of bringing families and schools into closer harmony.

Most recently, in America, Molnar and Lindquist (1989) have described a school-focused approach which involves classroom teachers and other school personnel using systemic techniques in the normal course of their work. Molnar and Lindquist's work is particularly apposite at the present time in Britain, coming as it does in the wake of the Elton Report (DES, 1989), since it takes as its focus the need to provide teachers with techniques for dealing with oppositional pupil behaviour of the type identified as being most prevalent in the national survey commissioned by the Elton Committee (Gray and Sime, 1989). These behaviours are termed 'oppositional' because they represent deliberate and repeated infringements of classroom rules which teachers impose in order to create, what they believe to be, the necessary conditions for effective teaching and learning to take place.

The main problem with the types of behavioural difficulties described here is their persistence and apparent resistance to the approaches which teachers most commonly use to oppose them (e.g. reasoning, punishment, ignoring, detention, discussion, withdrawal, referral to another teacher, withdrawal of privileges [see the Elton Report, DES, 1989, p.240]). These (essentially 'lineal') approaches, far from changing the problem behaviour, can serve to maintain and promote the behaviour they seek to alter. The ecosystemic approach of Molnar and Lindquist, however, seeks to offer teachers the means to change the problem behaviour, not by challenging the behaviour overtly, but by utilising the systemic principles which sustain interactional patterns. One of the major aims of their approach is to assist teachers in redefining oppositional behaviour in terms which lead both teacher and perpetrator to see the behaviour as co-operative or positive, rather than oppositional or negative. Deprived of a barrier against which to kick, and presented with a new and undesired rationale for the negative behaviour, the behaviour loses its original effect and is, therefore, made redundant.

The very act of developing a new perception of the negative behaviour can itself remove the teacher's desire to change the behaviour though, more often, it is the projection of this new perception which leads the pupil toward a conscious decision to change the behaviour pattern. Thus the pupil's determination to behave according to his/her own value system, and not to be merely obedient to the teacher's wishes, is employed by the teacher as a means of controlling the pupil's behaviour. For this reason the approach has been referred to as employing 'judo principles' (Mandel *et al.*, 1975). The key point is, however, that behaviour problems are resolved without loss of face and without the pupil surrendering behavioural autonomy. This makes the approach particularly appropriate to classrooms in which qualities of autonomy and self direction are valued, pupil traits which may be threatened by approaches to problem behaviour which demand the pupil's open surrender of autonomy in subservience to the teacher's authority.

As yet, there are no published examples of the use of such interventions in British schools. There is, however, a growing number of reports and articles describing the successful use of such strategies in American schools. Mandel *et al.* (1975) describe the successful use of such techniques with emotionally and behaviour disordered (EBD) pupils in a special school who swear and are belligerent towards teachers. Others describe the successful use of such techniques in mainstream schools with pupils who present physical aggression toward other pupils (Brown, 1986), tantrum behaviour (Amatea, 1988), fighting, in-school truancy, depression with suicidal tendencies (Williams and Weeks, 1984), and school phobia/school refusal (Hsia, 1984). Molnar and Lindquist (1989) also describe the use of these techniques with a wide range of behaviour problems commonly encountered in mainstream schools, such as: lack of attentiveness, chronic 'gossiping', apparent inability to settle down to work, failure to complete homework and classwork assignments, talking out of turn, interrupting the teacher and belligerence toward teachers and pupils. They also describe instances in which teachers employed the techniques successfully with problematic colleagues.

KEY COMPONENTS OF THE ECOSYSTEMIC APPROACH TO SCHOOL BEHAVIOUR PROBLEMS

Below is an exposition of some of the key features of the ecosystemic approach to school behaviour problems (see also Upton and Cooper, 1990):

1   Problem behaviour in the classroom does not originate from within the individual who displays the behaviour, but is a product of social interaction.

2   Interactional patterns may be conceptualised in simple or complex ways. The simple analysis is confined to here and now situations and will define a student's negative behaviour in terms of the interactions which immediately surround this behaviour. A complex analysis will take into account factors in the wider ecosystem, and explore purposes which the here and now behaviour might serve in other, related eco-systems. Such an analysis may relate oppositional behaviour in the classroom to interactional patterns in the student's family.

3   The cause of any instance of problem behaviour is part of a cyclical chain of actions and reactions between participants. Each event in the interactional chain is both a cause of ensuing events and the effect of preceding events. Student classroom behaviour which is defined as 'problematic' is always goal directed, and from the student's viewpoint it is understandable, rational, and above all, necessary. What appears problematic to the teacher may well be the solution to a problem for the student, for a sub-system in the classroom or school, or the student's family. Attempts to directly oppose goal-directed behaviour inevitably meet with resistance, and can, therefore, help to encourage the prob-lematic situation to continue. The repeated use of failed solutions, in this way, is often characteristic of apparently intractable systemic problems.

4   Intervention, based on an ecosystemic analysis, must recognise the contribution made to the interactional events surrounding a problem, by all participating parties. This emphasises the reflexive quality of the ecosystemic approach which requires teachers to analyse their own behaviour and its relation to the perceived problem. Teachers can only influence their students by eschewing confrontational approaches and entering into a co-operative relationship with them, in which the 'prob-lematic' behaviour is reconstructed in terms which are meaningful to both the student and the teacher (and members of significant sub-systems, such as family members, other students and school personnel, where appropriate) and which reveal one or more of the following things: (a) the goals served by the behaviour; (b) the inappropriateness, for the student, of the goals that are or may be served by the behaviour; and (c) alternative/more effective means of achieving the goals which the behaviour is perceived to serve.

In constructing a picture of a problem situation it is necessary for the teacher to establish awareness of his/her phenomenological interpretation of the situation, and to set this against those of others involved, particularly students. The teacher must identify in specific behavioural terms: (a) the precise nature of the problem as she/he sees it, in terms of repeating behavioural patterns, the times, places and individuals involved, (b) possible positive interpretations of the problem behaviour, and (c) how the situation will be different when improvement begins and after the problem is solved. This involves the teacher in a degree of self analysis, in which evidence for the existence of the problem is amassed and scrutinised, along with the teacher's behavioural expectations. Molnar and Lindquist (1989) describe this process as 'sleuthing'. A vital component of the process involves the teacher in seeking perspectives on the situation other than his/her own; particularly those of the students involved. Molnar and Lindquist suggest that teachers be alert to students' use of figurative language in their descriptions of problematic situations. Since it is through figurative language that we make personal sense of the reality around us, it follows that teachers will communicate more effectively with students if they make use of their figurative language, and use this as an exploratory tool in defining situations from the students' viewpoint. (It would seem to us also that this recognition of the importance of students' viewpoints has important implications for patterns of classroom interaction which suggest links between the ecosystemic approach and humanistic approaches to education.) Teachers must also be constantly alert to positive changes, however apparently insignificant, which occur in the classroom ecosystem, whether or not they appear to be related to the problem situation or not. Such minor changes may give rise to hitherto unthought of solutions.

Intervention

The chief characteristic of recurring problem situations is their apparent self-perpetuating inevitability. Individuals believe themselves to be behaving in the only rational way that is possible in the given circumstances. For instance, a teacher reprimands a pupil who disobeys her; the pupil responds to the reprimand with abuse; the teacher reprimands the pupil further; the pupil abuses the teacher further; and so on. Each is driven by the conviction that not to confront the other's reprimand/abuse is to accept the unacceptable. A distinguishing characteristic of ecosystemic intervention is the use of 'divergent explanations of problem behaviour' (Molnar and Lindquist, 1989, p.xv). Such divergent explanations seek to redefine problem situations so that conflict (or resistance) is seen as cooperation. This tenet holds true in any social ecosystem whether it be, for example, the interactional dyad of the pupil and teacher, the mesosystem (i.e. the interaction among systems) of family and school, or even super-power and super-power.

As has already been noted, behaviour which functions to maintain an individual's symptomatic condition can often be seen, from a systemic viewpoint, to be serving a goal elsewhere in the system. Power and Bartholomew (1985) present a case study, involving a student with learning and behaviour difficulties, in which parent–school enmity is seen to be a predominant factor. After a period of sustained conflict between the school and the family, a family therapist was brought in as consultant. The therapist developed the following interpretation of the situation. The student was seen by his teachers to be underachieving and his parents appeared to be using their son's difficulties as a diversion from their marital problems. The parents were able to unite with one another in their concern for their son's problems and this helped to prevent marital break-up. Consequently, the parents had a vested interest in maintaining their son's difficulties and did so by opposing the school's efforts to solve their son's problems through, for instance, over-protectiveness and encouraging him not to complete homework assignments. Teachers at the school responded to what they saw as family collusion by being unsympathetic towards the student and making unrealistic demands upon him. The school–family relationship was seen to be characterised by a pattern of symmetrical interaction, 'that is, one in which each party responds to what the other is doing in a similar way' (Power and Bartholomew, 1985, p.223). Such relationships are founded on constant competition for the dominant position. Thus, in the present case, the teachers' suggestion that the student's school problems were related to the family circumstances would be met by the counterclaim that the teachers were not working effectively. It is the nature of such relationships to escalate, leading to deeper entrenchment on both sides, with each party undermining the efforts made by the other to help the student. The chief loser here, ironically, is the student.

Clearly, such a conflict situation would be unlikely to produce a solution to the student's difficulties. The consultant family therapist proposed an intervention which sought to convert this symmetrical relationship into a complementary relationship. A complementary relationship is characterised by non-competitive interaction so that, for instance, dominance is met with passivity, anger with appeasement, and so on. The consultant persuaded the school personnel to be compliant with the parents' views at the next meeting and to adopt a subordinate role. When, during the meeting, the parents became hostile toward the school staff, the social worker took up the parental position and presented it in an exaggerated form, suggesting that their son should be relieved of all pressures in class. The parents responded to this in a conciliatory manner and for the first time they suggested that 'the teacher did have the right to place some expectations on the students in her class' (Power and Bartholomew, 1985, p.226). This was a point at which the parents and staff were in agreement for the first time. The deadlock was broken and an opportunity to develop a collaborative relationship was established. The eventual outcome of this case was that the parents and the school personnel agreed to recognise the primacy of each other in their respective domains. The teachers agreed not to pressurise the student in class and, instead of setting specific homework tasks in addition to classwork, they agreed to allow him to take uncompleted classwork tasks home. It was agreed that whether he completed the tasks at home was a matter for the parents to decide and the school would simply award the appropriate grade without placing any pressure on the student. By allowing the student to take classwork home, the school was enabling the parents to control the 'pressure' their son was placed under. This newly collaborative relationship between the school and the family also led to their accepting advice from a psychologist on aiding their son with stress management. Thus the student's therapeutic needs were met, as were the parents' needs for a collaborative activity with one another (i.e. as a diversion from their marital difficulties) and the school's position was also validated.

A key feature shared by ecosystemic intervention strategies, and demonstrated in the above example, is that, when they succeed, individuals change their behaviour and become more co-operative with others whilst retaining their sense of control over their own behaviour. For example, the parents in the case study, when faced with an overly compliant response, found that it was necessary, for their own purposes, to support the school position and to soften their dominant stance. They stated that they wanted the school to place a certain amount of pressure on their son, even though this had been a major source of disagreement earlier. This point emphasises the ecosystemic idea that it is the patterns of interaction among people which maintain problematic situations rather than the situation which appears to be the focus of the problem. The purpose of ecosystemic intervention techniques is to offer participants the means to break out of destructive cycles of interaction through the creation of new cycles. This is demonstrated repeatedly by Molnar and Lindquist (1989) in their exemplification of ecosystemic techniques for classroom teachers and other school personnel.

The archetypal ecosystemic technique, described by Molnar and Lindquist, is that of 'reframing'. The technique is based on four basic propositions: (a) we behave in accordance with the way in which we interpret problem situations; (b) there are often many different but equally valid interpretations of any given situation; (c) if we change our interpretation then we can change our behaviour: and (d) change in our behaviour will influence the perceptions and behaviour of others.

For example, a teacher may seek to reprimand a student in order to prevent him/her from repeatedly talking out of turn. The student, however, might persist with the deviant behaviour regardless of the increasing severity of the reprimands. Without knowing what that pupil's perception of the situation is the teacher is still able to effect change in the ecosystem by changing her own perceptions and behaviour. The teacher's behaviour is clearly based on the interpretation that talking out of turn is a deviant act. The reframing technique requires the teacher to seek a new, plausible and positive interpretation of the behaviour through the process of 'sleuthing' and then to behave in strict accordance with this, for it is essential that the reframing be feasible and believable in the eyes of the pupil. Such an interpretation might be that the student often interrupts the teacher in order to seek clarification for particular points made by the teacher. The behaviour is now defined as a positive service to the class as a whole.

For the intervention to be effective the teacher must behave in strict accordance with the reframing. In order to do this the 'symptom prescription' technique (Molnar and Lindquist, 1989) might be used. This involves the teacher encouraging the student to perform the symptomatic behaviour in revised circumstances. The teacher might suggest to the student that she/he increase the frequency of interruption in order to optimise the value of the service it provides.

The successful outcome of such intervention would be that a situation of conflict has now become one of co-operation. As with the antagonistic parents referred to above, the apparent concession by a former adversary may give rise to complementary concessions. On the other hand, it could be said that control of the problematic behaviour has now passed from the student to the teacher. Where the behaviour may have been perceived in the past as a means by which the student gained control over the teacher (by 'winding him/her up'), it has now become a means by which the teacher exerts control over the student. In any event talking out of turn is now redundant as a tool for engaging in conflict; to do so now is in fact perceived as an act of co-operation. The likelihood is that the student will cease the behaviour and possibly take up another form of behaviour which achieves the initial goal of the interrupting behaviour.

Molnar and Lindquist provide many examples in which interventions of this sort succeed and they repeatedly suggest, on the basis of anecdotal reports of teachers using such approaches, that the seed of co-operation that is planted in such situations often has a transforming effect on the quality of interpersonal relationships involved. Students with whom teachers have experienced difficulty in forming co-operative relationships become more amenable and generally much easier to get along with. Such observations require careful consideration and experimental scrutiny. As they stand, however, these observations suggest a number of interesting hypotheses as to the effect of ecosystemic approaches on the social climate of the classroom which would seem to be in line with research which has shown the considerable influence of teacher expectations on pupil performance and behaviour (for example Hargreaves *et al.*, 1975).

CONCLUSION: TOWARDS A NEW EDUCATIONAL PERSPECTIVE

An ecosystemic approach seeks to define behaviour problems in schools in terms of the interactional systems which maintain and promote behaviour. This approach rejects ways of conceptualising behaviour problems which see the problem in terms of a quality or defect of the individual. As such, the ecosystemic approach is in keeping with the wealth of research evidence which describes the ways in which schools and teachers unwittingly engage in the construction of 'deviant' pupils (Keddie, 1971; Sharp and Green, 1975; Hargreaves *et al.*, 1975; Reid, 1985). These and other writers argue that it is the quality of interpersonal interaction between teachers and pupils in many of our schools that produces students who are disaffected and actively resist their teachers in return for what they see as the degradation and ill treatment that characterises the daily routines in many schools (Hargreaves, 1967; Rosser and Harre, 1976; Woods, 1976; Tattum, 1982; Schostak, 1983). These writers draw on the testimony of pupils to make the case that disruptive behaviour in schools can often be seen as a rational response to intolerable circumstances.

The ecosystemic approach offers a mechanism for analysing and changing interactional patterns that can be employed by individuals at the dyadic level as well as at larger institutional levels. The vital importance of the school–family interactive system which has long been seen as an important area for development in British education, particularly in relation to learning and behavioural difficulties (DES, 1978; Reynolds and Sullivan, 1979; Galloway, 1985; Galloway and Goodwin, 1987; DES, 1989), is also recognised by this approach and practical measures for overcoming some of the difficulties encountered in this area are suggested.

In these important areas the ecosystemic approach can be seen to indicate new avenues for research and application. It is envisaged that such work would provide a valuable addition to that which is already being done by some advocates of behavioural approaches (for example Wheldall and Merrett, 1984; Wheldall, 1987; Wheldall and Glynn, 1989) who are concerned to promote the development of learning environments which are more responsive to the needs of school students through the sensitisation of teachers and parents to the influence they can have on the behaviour of students.

In looking to the future of the ecosystemic approach and its application to British education, we see certain important contextual factors of which account must be taken. The first is what we see as the humanistic tradition in British education which can be traced back to the early writings of A.S. Neill (Neill, 1916), through the child-centred movement of the 1960s (DES, 1967) the development of student-initiated learning approaches (Barnes, 1976) and into the contemporary concern for democratic schooling (Fletcher *et al.*, 1985; Harber and Meighan, 1989). In a recent micro-sociological study, Cronk (1987) has shown how a humanistic approach to classroom behaviour problems can lead to an improvement in students' classroom behaviour and lesson involvement. Central to Cronk's approach is the importance attached to the sharing of phenomenological constructs of the classroom situation between pupils and teachers. This clearly relates to Molnar and Lindquist's (1989) concept of 'sleuthing'. We suggest that the effectiveness of such 'sleuthing', the aim of which is to gain an under-standing of students' phenomenological worlds, would be enhanced if the 'sleuths' were trained in some of the counselling skills of humanistic psychology which involve the development of empathy through the exer-cise of skills such as active listening, reflection and paraphrase (Rogers, 1980; Mearns and Thorne, 1988). The absence of empathic understanding between teachers and students would seem, from a reading of the literature on school behaviour problems referred to above, to be a major factor in the development and maintenance of behaviour problems. The use of empathy, by teachers, would add to the reflexive quality of the ecosystemic approach with regard to teacher behaviour by encouraging teachers continually to analyse the experience of schooling from the student's standpoint.

A second contextual matter relates to the role of the mainstream class-room teacher in British schools. Concern has been expressed in recent years about the way in which support staff, delegated to mainstream schools to act as consultants to mainstream teachers in the support of pupils with special educational needs, have been increasingly used by mainstream schools in the role of peripatetic specialist teachers. Galloway and Good-win (1987) have suggested that this situation has had the reverse effect to that of its original intention and has resulted in the 'de-skilling' of main-stream teachers in the special educational needs area. This can be seen in the broader context of increased specialisation in the teaching force in which teachers' roles become evermore precisely defined in terms of specialist skills and responsibilities. Galloway (1985) has suggested that the pastoral effectiveness of some schools has been undermined by the development of separate pastoral systems which have the twin effects of identifying certain teachers as having specialist pastoral responsibilities, whilst excluding other 'non-specialist' teachers from the performance of pastoral functions. In the face of such tendencies toward 'de-skilling', we suggest that the ecosystemic approach offers skills which mainstream teachers could develop through in-service training, as Molnar and Lindquist (1989) have suggested.

Whilst the examples of ecosystemic interventions described by Molnar and Lindquist would appear to be well within the capablilities of appropriately trained mainstream teachers, those joint systems interventions which involve school and family would clearly remain within the province of the specialist family therapist. We would suggest, however, that the training of teachers in ecosystemic approaches will make teachers more aware of the potential value of family therapy and, therefore, more likely to seek the support of family therapists in the context of the type of outreach model described by Taylor and Dowling (1986) and Dowling and Taylor (1989).

Molnar and Lindquist (1989) provide a range of techniques which they claim can be easily assimilated by teachers who can use them autonomously and to great effect. One of the key features of the ecosystemic approach is a recognition of the power that can be derived from different perspectives on a situation. With this in mind, it would seem that the ecosystemic approach might develop in the context of staff support groups (as recommended by the Elton Committee) with access to a specialist family therapist (and/or educational psychologist trained in family therapy), who could perform the dual roles of professional supervisor and training consultant. Peer group support would facilitate the development of new perspectives on difficult situations and have valuable social implications for teachers who often feel professionally isolated in these matters. The availablity of a specialist consultant would also help teachers to decide when it was appropriate to hand cases over to specialist therapists. The effectiveness of this approach, however, still needs to be established, as does the feasibility of staff–peer support groups. Clearly, the next step in developing the ecosystemic approach in a British context will involve research into these areas.

REFERENCES

Amatea, E. (1988) 'Brief systemic interventions with school behavior problems: a case of temper tantrums', *Psychology in the Schools* 2: 174–83.
Barnes, D. (1976) *From Communication to Curriculum*, Harmondsworth: Penguin.
Bateson, G. (1972) *Steps to an Ecology of Mind*, New York: Chandler.
—— (1979) *Mind and Nature: a necessary unity*, New York: Dutton.
Bridge, S. and Luke, S. (1989) *Blackstone's Guide to the Children Act 1989*, London: Blackstone.
Brown, J. (1986) 'The use of paradoxical intervention with oppositional behavior in the classroom', *Psychology in the Schools* 21: 77–81.

Campion, J. (1985) *The Child in Context: family systems theory in educational psychology*, London: Methuen.

Cooper, P. (1989) 'Respite, relationships and re-signification: a study of the effects of residential schooling on pupils with emotional and behavioural difficulties, with particular reference to the pupils' perspective', unpublished doctoral thesis, University of Birmingham.

Cronk, K. (1987) *Teacher–Pupil Conflict in Secondary Schools*, London: Falmer.

de Shazer, S. (1982) *Patterns of Brief Family Therapy: an ecosystemic approach*, New York: Guildford.

—— (1985) *Keys to Solution*, New York: Norton.

DES (1967) *Children and their Primary Schools (The Plowden Report)*, London: HMSO.

—— (1978) *Special Educational Needs (The Warnock Report)*, London: HMSO.

—— (1989) *Discipline in Schools (The Elton Report)*, London: HMSO.

Dowling, E. and Osborne, E. (eds) (1985) *The Family and the School*, London: Routledge & Kegan Paul.

Dowling, E. and Taylor, D. (1989) 'The clinic goes to school: lessons learnt', *Maladjustment and Therapeutic Education* 7: 24–9.

Fletcher, C., Caron, M. and Williams, W. (1985) *Schools on Trial*, Milton Keynes: Open University Press.

Galloway, D. (1985) 'Pastoral care and school effectiveness', in D. Reynolds (ed.) *Studying School Effectiveness*, London: Falmer Press.

Galloway, D. and Goodwin, C. (1987) *The Education of Disturbing Children*, London: Longman.

Gray, J. and Sime, S. (1989) 'Teachers and discipline: a report for the committee of enquiry into discipline in schools by Sheffield University', Appendix D of *Discipline in Schools (The Elton Report)*, London: HMSO.

Harber, C. and Meighan, R. (eds) (1989) *The Democratic School*, Ticknall: Education Now.

Hargreaves, D. (1967) *Social Relations in a Secondary School*, London: Routledge & Kegan Paul.

Hargreaves, D., Hester, S. and Mellor, F. (1975) *Deviance in Classrooms*, London: Routledge & Kegan Paul.

Hsia, H. (1984) 'Structural and strategic approaches to school phobia/school refusal', *Psychology in the Schools* 21: 360–7.

Keddie, N. (1971) 'Classroom knowledge', in M. Young (ed.) *Knowledge and Control*, London: Collier-Macmillan.

Lindquist, B., Molnar, A. and Brauchmann, L. (1987) 'Working with school related problems without going to school: considerations for systemic practice', *Journal of Strategic and Systemic Therapies* 6: 44–50.

Mandel, H., Weizmann, F., Millan, B., Greenhow, J. and Speers, D. (1975) 'Reaching emotionally disturbed children: "judo" principles in remedial education', *American Journal of Orthopsychiatry* 45: 867–74.

Mearns, D. and Thorne, B. (1988) *Person Centred Counselling in Action*, London: Sage.

Minuchin, S. (1974) *Families and Family Therapy*, Cambridge, Mass.: Harvard University Press.

Molnar, A. and Lindquist, B. (1989) *Changing Problem Behavior in Schools*, San Francisco: Jossey Bass.

Neill, A.S. (1916) *A Dominie's Log*, London: Herbert Jenkins.

Okun, B. (1984) 'Family therapy and the schools', in B. Okun (ed.) *Family Therapy with School Related Problems*, Rockville: Aspen.

Parsons, T. (1951) *The Social System*, Glencoe, Kentucky: Free Press.

Power, T. and Bartholomew, K. (1985) 'Getting uncaught in the middle: a case study in family-school system consultation', *School Psychology Review* 14: 2, 222–9.

Reid, K. (1985) *Truancy and School Absenteeism*, London: Hodder & Stoughton.

Reynolds, D. and Sullivan, M. (1979) 'Bringing schools back in', in L. Barton and R. Meighan, (eds) *Schools, Pupils and Deviance*, Nafferton: Nafferton Books.

Rogers, C. (1980) *A Way of Being*, Boston: Houghton-Mifflin.

Rosser, E. and Harre, R. (1976) 'The meaning of trouble', in M. Hammersley and P. Woods (eds) *The Process of Schooling*, London: Routledge & Kegan Paul.

Schostak, J. (1983) *Maladjusted Schooling*, London: Falmer.

Selvini-Palazzoli, M., Boscolo, L., Cecchin, G. and Prata, G. (1973) *Paradox and Counterparadox*, New York: Aronson.

Sharp, R. and Green, A. (1975) *Education and Social Control*, London: Routledge & Kegan Paul.

Smith, A. (1978) 'Encountering the family system in school-related problems', *Psychology in the Schools* 15: 379–86.

Speed, B. (1984) 'Family therapy: an update', *Association of Child Psychology and Psychiatry Newsletter* 6: 2–14.

Tattum, D. (1982) *Disruptive Pupils in Schools and Units*, Chichester: Wiley.

Taylor, D. and Dowling, E. (1986) 'The clinic goes to school: setting up an outreach service', *Maladjustment and Therapeutic Education* 4: 90–8.

Upton, G. and Cooper, P. (1990) 'A new perspective on behaviour problems in schools: the ecosystemic approach', *Maladjustment and Therapeutic Education* 8: 3–18.

von Bertalanffy, L. (1950) 'The theory of open systems in physics and biology', *Science* 3: 25–9.

——— (1968) *General System Theory*, New York: Brazillier.

Wheldall, K. (ed.) (1987) *The Behaviourist in the Classroom*, London: Allen & Unwin.

Wheldall, K. and Glynn, T. (1989) *Effective Classroom Learning: a behavioural interactionist approach to teaching*, Oxford: Basil Blackwell.

Wheldall, K. and Merrett, F. (1984) *Positive Teaching: the behavioural approach*, London: Allen & Unwin.

Williams, J. and Weeks, G. (1984) 'The use of paradoxical techniques in a school setting', *The American Journal of Family Therapy* 12: 47–57.

Woods, P. (1976) 'Having a laugh: an antidote to schooling', in M. Hammersley and P. Woods (eds) *The Process of Schooling*, London: Routledge & Kegan Paul.

Worden, M. (1981) 'Classroom behavior as a function of the family system', *The School Counsellor* 8: 178–88.

8 Good relationships and classroom management skills

Nigel Hastings

At a time when educational studies and the disciplines from which they draw are deemed to be of marginal relevance to the training of teachers, it is encouraging, if ironic, that an important government enquiry should find so much of value in research and training materials emanating from these areas. Satisfying though this is for all who have argued against the wholesale expunging of educational studies from teacher education, the publication of the Elton Report (DES, 1989) and the government's adoption of some of its recommendations relating to teacher education and training raise further questions and matters requiring attention.

Among the 138 recommendations of the Report are a number which relate to the training of teachers in 'group management skills'. It is suggested that this vital aspect of professional competence receives insufficient attention within initial teacher training courses and recommendations are made about the ways in which this situation should be rectified. The evidence from this country and elsewhere certainly suggests that classroom behaviour is one of the main areas of concern of beginning teachers (Veenman, 1987). The Committee's advice has been acted upon; the Council for the Accreditation of Teacher Education (CATE) now requires classroom management skills to be explicitly taught and assessed on initial teacher training courses. The Elton Committee also recommended that 'group management skills' should be a priority area for training for serving teachers. Again, this advice has been acted upon and, with effect from April 1990, funds have been made available through the Local Education Authority Training Grants Scheme (LEATGS) for the provision of in-service training.

The design and delivery of training, particularly in the in-service context, will need to attend to both the evidence on which Elton draws and to the experiences and frameworks which serving teachers bring to bear on the issue. Most teachers claim expertise in managing classroom behaviour and a great many people who are not teachers are not reticent in prescribing how it should be done. It is an issue on which almost anyone will offer an opinion and advice. The evidence cited to justify these prescriptions is, generally, experience. The problem, of course, is that different people offer different solutions: they identify different sorts of practices and qualities as being important as a consequence of differing experiences.

The Elton Report is enormously helpful in this context. Not only does it draw proper attention to the degree of influence that teachers and schools can have on pupil behaviour, it also identifies particular features of teaching strategy and school organisation which serve to minimise disruption and to promote good behaviour. The evidence on which the Committee draws, however, is from the now relatively substantial body of systematic research conducted in this country and elsewhere. The problem with research evidence is that, on the whole, it tends to be dispersed, published in inaccessible places and written in language which is equally inaccessible for the great majority of teachers.

The great joy of the Elton Report is that it draws together this evidence and provides an exceptionally readable, readily available digest of the important research evidence in the area. It highlights those aspects of classroom management and school organisation which have been identified by systematic research as being associated with lower levels of disruption. Many of these elements, of course, are those which individual teachers' experience had led them to identify, but some are not.

The issue with which this chapter is centrally concerned is the relationship between everyday staffroom explanations of the conditions necessary for good behaviour in schools and classes, and the elements identified by the research on which Elton draws. Training, especially for experienced teachers, which does not enable clear links to be drawn between these two will be unlikely to be effective. In order to explore this issue we need to examine each in turn, beginning with teachers' ideas.

'GOOD RELATIONSHIPS'

'Starting where the learner is' expresses an old but none the less valuable maxim in training and educational contexts. Teachers have a whole range of explanations and prescriptions for troublesome behaviour in schools – as do many outside the profession. The great majority of them, of course, are likely to be very sound. The problem with these explanations and prescriptions is that they tend to be articulated at a fairly high level of generality. One rather common explanation is that 'it's all to do with relationships'. The attendant prescription is 'establish a good relationship with them and you won't have any trouble'. As advice to a teacher who is encountering difficulty, this is rarely enlightening or enabling – not because it is wrong, but because it is not clear what he/she should now do.

Good relationships between teachers and pupils are important: few would question this. Her Majesty's Inspectorate of Schools (HMI) endorses this in their claim that one of the factors most often associated with good behaviour is 'good relationships with mutual respect between teachers and pupils' (DES, 1987, p.3). But what is a 'good relationship' and, more usefully, how do you create one where it is currently absent? An answer to the first of these questions often comes in the form of 'treating pupils with respect', 'behaving courteously towards them', 'valuing what they have to say', etc. While unobjectionable, such an answer does little to inform the second, and arguably more important, question of how to create a good relationship. If the notion of 'good relationships' is to be built on in training, it has to be subject to some clarification and analysis. A good beginning can be made by examining the use of the construct in a rather unusual context.

Over a number of years, I have been struck by the way in which teachers following courses in behavioural classroom management have accounted for or described the effects of their efforts. In the typical case, the teacher brings about a marked improvement in the behaviour of one or more children through the use of contingent praise. Rather than explain the change in terms of 'having applied contingent reinforcement', the explanation that is often given is 'What has *really* changed is my relationship with him/her/them'. Rather than dismiss this as 'woolly romanticism' or as being 'non-behavioural', it is worth examining what has happened in so many of these cases and to see how change in behaviour might relate to the perception of an improved relationship.

By introducing changes to their patterns of interaction with children, teachers often find that children's behaviour also changes. Having started from a position where they felt that little that they did seemed to have any effect, teachers come to feel that they and their actions have consequences: children's behaviour is affected. The children are in a position where they might well feel similarly. Prior to their teacher changing his/her strategy, the only occasions on which many of these children regularly and predictably elicited their teacher's attention was when being troublesome. When they worked, their teachers were inclined to 'leave well alone' and, in effect, ignore them. Under the 'new regime', their teachers also respond, but in a distinctly different (i.e. pleasant) way, when they are working or in other ways behaving appropriately.

Having begun wilfully to acknowledge positive behaviour, the teacher has created a situation in which there is a greater degree of mutual contingency between his/her behaviour and the pupil's. The behaviour of each has come to have a greater and more predictable range of consequences in the behaviour of the other. This increased reciprocity in behaviour may be an important element in understanding what many of the teachers who have successfully undertaken this sort of intervention might mean by 'improved relationships'.

In a good relationship each party feels that they are important to the other and that the other is important to them. They feel that what they say and do matters. This feeling does not arise out of thin air, however. It is generally experienced because a reciprocal contingency actually exists in behaviour. One feature of a good relationship is that each party's behaviour is affected by the other's in both pleasing and, at least potentially, displeasing ways. Each has the experience of their behaviour being of consequence to the other – because they see that to be the case. A relationship is not described as being 'good' if each party's behaviour does not influence, and is not influenced by, the behaviour of the other in satisfying ways, or if there is an acute asymmetry of influence. In a 'good relationship', each feels that what they do affects the other and that what the other does is of consequence to them – and each is right!

Central to this, admittedly speculative, discussion of good teacher–pupil relationship has been the contingency of behaviour between the two and the experience each has of being of significance to the other in their actions. Now, if it is true that good teacher–pupil relationships are important for discipline, and if it is also true that good teacher–pupil relationships demonstrate the kind of mutual contingency in behaviour that has been suggested, then the qualities which the Elton Committee describes as being the elements of good classroom management ought to reflect this mutual contingency.

GOOD CLASSROOM MANAGEMENT

From a review of the research evidence, the Elton Report identifies the following as components of group management skills:

* knowing pupils names, interests, etc.;
* planning and organisation of lessons, resources and the physical environment together with flexibility within what has been planned;
* frequent scanning of the class;
* emphasising the positive, praising good behaviour as well as good work;
* clear rules and expectations for behaviour;
* sparing and consistent use of punishments.

The Report particularly emphasises the need for teachers to attend to the effects, often unintended, of their own behaviour (stance, tone of voice, etc.) on pupils and to the ways in which they can use their own behaviour to good effect.

Although the Report makes little explicit reference to research, it is clear from the elements described above that evidence gathered in research such as that reported in Galton *et al.*, (1980); Kounin (1970); Mortimore *et al.*, (1986); Reynolds (1982); Rutter *et al.*, (1979); Wheldall and Glynn (1989) and Wragg (1984) has been carefully scrutinised.

While the detail of these elements is very important in the context of providing training, it is also useful to step back and consider the picture of the model classroom which emerges from the list. It is of a classroom in which the teacher is differentially responsive, in relatively consistent ways, to both desirable and troublesome behaviour, acknowledging and encouraging the positive and reproving the negative. Good behaviour and bad is clearly defined and both are responded to; the learning environment is planned, organised and yet responsive to unexpected things that happen or unexpected questions that children might raise. An environment which is responsive to pupils in these ways is one which is likely to enhance both teachers' and pupils' feeling of significance for the other.

The Elton Report is concerned not only with the ways in which individual teachers can create an environment in which disruptive behaviour is likely to be minimised but also with the ways in which schools, as whole institutions, can do the same. In considering this, the Committee again reviewed the research evidence concerned with the organisational features of schools which are associated with lower rates of disruption. As for the classroom, the Report identifies a number of features of school organisation which are associated with better behaviour. Reynolds (1982) offers a similar, though more qualified, list. Both construct an image of the ideal school as one which is responsive to pupil's behaviour in relatively consistent ways. This model school acknowledges and rewards the behaviours it has corporately decided to encourage and develop and it admonishes those it wants to discourage. If a school responds in relatively consistent, and therefore predictable, ways to pupils' positive and disruptive behaviour, it provides the type of environment which is most likely to engender a feeling among pupils that what they do matters and has consequences.

A FRAMEWORK FOR TRAINING

It appears that the notion of 'good teacher–pupil relationships', a concept which is so central to thinking from the staffroom to HMI, has considerable potential to inform the design and delivery of training in classroom management skills if it is interpreted in the way outlined above. The particular interpretation is important, however. Good relationships are sometimes referred to as if they are a prerequisite for good classroom management. This is not a helpful perspective. However, by viewing relationships as a product of patterns of interaction, and by considering 'good relationships' as arising from contingency in behaviour, some useful links can be drawn between the research evidence about behaviour, the important component skills of group management identified by Elton and beliefs about the significance of 'good relationships'.

Teachers are surely right: good relationships with pupils are important. But it is only when we clarify what actually happens in a good relationship and are able to say what such a relationship looks like from the point of view of an observer, it is only when we can say what teachers who have good relationships with their pupils actually do, that advocating good relationships becomes a useful activity. Reciprocal contingency in behaviour between teacher and pupils holds promise in this respect and could prove to be a useful organising principle for the design of training for teachers. It links the mysterious and romantic idea of 'good relationships' to the hard-headed but empirically justified prescriptions which the Elton Report offers for classroom management skills and their development.

REFERENCES

DES (1987) *Educational Observed 5, Good Behaviour and Discipline in Schools*, London: HMSO.
—— (1989) *Discipline in Schools (The Elton Report)*, London: HMSO.
Galton, M., Simon, B. and Croll, P. (1980) *Progress and Performance in the Primary Classroom*, London: Routledge & Kegan Paul.
Kounin, J.S. (1970) *Discipline and Group Management in Classrooms*, New York: Holt, Rinehart & Winston.
Mortimore, P., Sammons, P., Stoll, L., Lewis, D. and Ecob, R. (1986) *The Junior School Project. Main Report Parts A, B, C and Technical Appendices*, London: Research and Statistics Branch, ILEA.
Reynolds, D. (1982) 'The search for effective schools', *School Organisation* 2: 215–37.
Rutter, M., Maugham, B., Mortimore, P. and Ousten, J. (1979) *Fifteen Thousand Hours*, London: Open Books.
Veenman, S. (1987) 'Problems as perceived by new teachers', in N. Hastings and J. Schwieso (eds) *New Directions in Educational Psychology 2: Behaviour and motivation in the classroom*, London: Falmer.
Wheldall, K. and Glynn, T. (1989) *Effective Classroom Leaning: a behavioural interactionist approach to teaching*, Oxford: Basil Blackwell.
Wragg, E.C. (ed.) (1984) *Classroom Teaching Skills*, London: Croom Helm.

9   *Discipline in schools*:
A concluding review

Josh Schwieso

The reviewer asked to provide a commentary on, or critique of, contributions to a volume such as this faces some tough decisions. Is each chapter to be addressed in turn, reviewing its strengths and weaknesses? Should the reviewer concentrate on what had been omitted, assuming that the reader had no further need to be reminded of contributors' manifest strengths? But then the task is not one of judging suitability for publication. Mark Anthony might have 'come to bury Caesar not to praise him' but that was hardly what the editor or readers would desire. In the end I decided not to consider the papers sequentially but rather to pull out issues that seemed to call for particular comment and development.

AN AREA OF WIDESPREAD AGREEMENT: SCHOOLS ARE CRUCIAL

What question were the various papers meant to be addressing? Wheldall, in his preface to this book, refers to considered responses to the Elton Report, and saw these responses as a series of different psychological models for tackling the problem. The models are certainly different but how different? One cannot help but be impressed by the degree to which participants seem to have agreed with one another. All accept that the key place that classroom misbehaviour should, and indeed can, be tackled is in the school itself. This is worthy of emphasis. Twenty-five years ago Jenks' book *Inequality* (1975) marked the zenith of the belief that schools made little, if any, difference in educational terms. Now the pendulum has swung the other way. However, although experts seem to be in agreement as to this point, it is questionable whether teachers are so convinced (see, for example Chapter 1). Two decades of being told one is ineffective and feeling undervalued may take more than this Report to overcome.

In Chapter 1, Bennett notes that some journalists regarded the fact that the majority of Elton's recommendations were directed towards teachers and schools as prima-facie evidence that schools were the prime culprits over indiscipline. The same sort of reasoning no doubt would impel us to infer that reports on the treatment of AIDS, being directed mainly to doctors, demonstrate the culpability of the medical profession in causing the disease! In a more serious vein this focus on teacher responsibility is an inevitable consequence of a renewed belief that schools do make a difference, in terms of both academic and social behaviour, and should therefore be given a guarded welcome by those concerned with teacher education.

Perhaps one might register some slight dissent from the contributors' near obsession with the school. Elton, after all, addresses itself to the whole spectrum of those responsible for pupils, reaching even to matters of television programming. Upton and Cooper note, in passing, that school misbehaviour can reflect current home conflicts, and Glynn addresses the issue of parental responsibility (also dear to the heart of many Conservative Party thinkers). However, if one is permitted a truism, schooling occurs within specific societal arrangements. The various London school projects (Rutter *et al*., 1979; Mortimore *et al*., 1988) never claimed that catchment areas had no impact on pupils' outcomes, but merely that schools could have an impact independent of these intake variables. What curricula are seen as relevant must depend upon the political, economic and cultural situation. To echo the (much maligned) Bernstein (1970), 'Education cannot compensate for society'.

MISBEHAVIOUR AND ACADEMIC FAILURE

Colin Smith (Chapter 4) tackles an issue that is not neglected by Elton but which, nevertheless, bears repetition; if the teacher is on-task in terms of the academic content and presentation, many discipline problems are far less likely to occur. Smith is primarily concerned with special needs and, in particular, the place of support teaching, but the main thrust of his article has relevance for all pupils. But however obvious the point, its application may not be so easy. Teachers do not control all aspects of the curriculum. No one doubts that dull presentation and poor teaching can turn pupils off. But the opposite must be true; that there is a limit to the degree that teachers can motivate students in areas which have no appeal to them (unless, that is, high levels of extrinsic reinforcement are to be applied). Will the National Curriculum, and its associated testing, prove sufficiently motivating?

The degree to which good teaching pre-empts inappropriate behaviour is also raised when one considers the nature of classroom discipline. In addition to those social behaviours without which classroom learning cannot occur there is a range of others which, although necessary in some general sense, do not have the same immediacy (changing into outdoor shoes and wiping one's feet when coming in from the playground on a wet day for example). Now clearly appropriate social behaviour in school is valued, not merely because it is instrumental in facilitating academic learning, but because it is a goal in its own right, as preparation for life in society. Be that as it may, it would seem that a great deal of personal scruffiness could be perfectly compatible with being a model learner (some top academics, for example, seem to have peculiarly disorganised personal lives in my experience). Hence, good teaching cannot be expected to eliminate certain types of perennial classroom problems.

TRIED AND TESTED TECHNIQUES?

The centrality of schools is not all that the various authors seem to agree on. Despite the fact that the psychological models represented include behavioural psychology, family therapy, systems theory and attribution theory, there is considerable consensus as to what sorts of strategies are called for. Action needs to be taken at three levels; the whole school, the classroom and in terms of handling individual pupils. Teaching and curricula must be of an appropriate level for each pupil. Teachers must receive more training in classroom management techniques and those techniques should focus on the use of positive controls. Perhaps this unanimity should not surprise us. In his preface, Wheldall remarks that he and his colleagues initially challenged the value of the Elton Committee of Enquiry. For them, what was needed was the implementation of empirically tried and tested techniques of classroom management rather than yet another official Report. Whether or not that was so, the Elton Report, and these chapters, have at least served to publicly vindicate Wheldall's optimism concerning positive approaches.

'Positive approaches'? Herein surely is the Elton Report's most important implication. Without directly saying so, the Report effectively endorses the main thrust, as well as many of the particular practices, of behavioural approaches to classroom management as, indeed, do most of the papers collected in this volume. Given that, it is very right and proper that the behavioural model, one of the best researched, and arguably the most effective frameworks for classroom management, is here represented by the work of Wheldall and Merrett. Behavioural approaches in education have been used in Britain since the 1970s but, without disparaging the pioneering efforts of educational psychologists such as John Presland or

Roger Burland, it is Kevin Wheldall and Frank Merrett who must take much of the credit for their considerable body of research and the wide-spread dissemination of behavioural approaches amongst British teachers and educationalists.

Given their limited brief, Wheldall and Merrett quite rightly concern themselves primarily with the role of behavioural psychology in assisting the classroom teacher to achieve social order. But it is surely in order to remind ourselves that behavioural psychology is concerned first and foremost with learning, regardless of the particular content or context. There are extensive applications of the behavioural approach to curriculum design and remedial teaching, for example Portage or DISTAR.

Most of the contributors discuss approaches to school and classroom management which sit quite comfortably with positive teaching (for example Burden's systems approach). Cooper and Upton alone offer a clear alternative to the behavioural model (although they argue that it is not incompatible with behavioural approaches). They believe teachers should be trained to apply insights from family therapy to the school situation. One might ask what would lead teachers to prefer what is, as the authors admit, a relatively untried enterprise to one that has amply proved its worth. Even on paper it seems to be a moot point as to whether family therapy has any greater potential than behavioural psychology. Applied behaviour analysis, as Wheldall and Merrett point out, fully acknowledges the role that relationships between actors in a social situation play in maintaining appropriate and inappropriate behaviour and has always emphasised the function that behaviour, however inappropriate from an adult viewpoint, must have for the child.

Both Wheldall and Merrett, and Cooper and Upton, make use of the prefix 'eco-'. The source of this metaphor is of course biology. For Cooper and Upton an individual's behaviour 'is the product of on-going interaction between environmental influences and internal motivations...both constrained by and a constraining force upon the behaviour and development of other organisms'. For Wheldall and Glynn (1989, p.27) ecological factors are 'more global aspects of the classroom environment' (for example heating, lighting, furniture). In the first case then the term invites us to consider interdependencies and reciprocal influences, in the latter it appears to be no more than a convenient term by which to distinguish one set of antecedent or setting events from another. I am not altogether happy about Wheldall and Glynn's usage since it does not appear to carry any of the cybernetic implications that Cooper and Upton's usage does, and which seem to be integral to the original, biological meaning of the term. But even in the case of family therapy one wonders what the invoking of environmental models actually means. Making links to theoretical perspectives from other disciplines no doubt conveys the feeling that one is making conceptual progress, but it is far from clear that social relationships are the same as biological systems (would it be true, for example, that only the fittest social relationships survive). The nub of the issue, surely, is that any action of mine has the potential to affect other people. 'Relationships' are stable patterns of mutual influence. In order to change a behaviour it is important – perhaps vital – to consider the relationship(s) within which it occurs. Conversely, as Hastings points out, in order to change a relationship it is important to consider the behaviours which comprise it. Does one need any further theoretical or terminological baggage?

RATIONALITY, TEACHING AND DISCIPLINE

Underlying the areas of general agreement are some deeper issues which, perhaps rightly, the individual contributors do not address. Bennett reminds us that the committee, in one respect, failed insofar as the much-exercised question of whether things were getting worse on the discipline front proved to be incapable of being answered. The data were simply not there. This absence surely calls for comment, just as the dog's failure to bark does in the Sherlock Holmes story. Given that school discipline must be one of the longest standing concerns of the teaching profession it really does seem strange that relevant data are so thin on the ground! How can this be?

One possibility is that the decline in standards of conduct may have been one of those 'facts' too obvious to need proof. Thus Merrett and Wheldall note (1987, p.37) that the increasing insubordination of the young is a perennial theme in Western culture, a theme which is surely closely related to the wider myth of social disintegration that conservative writers have held from at least the seventeenth century (Pearson, 1983).

However, the matter may be more serious. It is possible to argue that the act of teaching has been to a considerable degree a fact free activity. Those records that do exist are largely to do with the academic behaviour of pupils rather than with classroom discipline. (The Elton Report, to its credit, calls for schools and LEAs to commence serious record keeping on disruptive incidents.) The fact remains that currently there is no strong tradition for empirical data accumulation. Why?

It is an academic commonplace that Max Weber saw the rationalisation of life as a crucial feature in the emergence of modern Western European society. This rationalisation involves not only the selection of appropriate means by which to affect one's environment, but also a rationality of choice; the selection of suitable goals with regard to one's values and the engaging in rational arguments to support those values (see, for example, Brubaker, 1984, p.36). This practical rationality can be said to underlie modern science. More importantly for our purpose is the related assumption that human behaviour is equally as amenable to study and to rational manipulation as is the physical world. From this follows the emergence of social science and its incorporation into programmes of vocational education such as teacher training courses.

Herein lies the rub. Just as there is a strong anti-scientific element in modern culture so it is even more certain that there is a strong anti-social science element, resistant to the very idea that interpersonal behaviour can ever become the subject of technique or that institutions can be evaluated on social–scientific grounds. This hostility to educational 'studies' (as these social science contributions to teacher training are called) has considerable support amongst many of the intellectuals that comprise what is called the New Right (see, for example, the recent pamphlet from the Centre for Policy Studies (Lawlor, 1990) advocating the closing of teacher training courses). It is implicit in moves by the DES and the Council for the Accreditation of Teacher Education (CATE) to increase the subject content of teacher education at the expense of educational studies. Amongst teachers it is expressed in various ways; in a contempt for 'mere theory', in the call for more time in schools during teacher training (as if the prospect of forty years in the classroom were not enough!), in the notion that only experience and innate talent are called for in order to be a good teacher, and in those interviewees for B.Ed. courses, who place an extraordinary premium on 'liking children' (as compared to, say, educating them!). Like any impatience with 'academic' concerns this tends to lead to a contempt for data too.

This distaste for hard data has some surprising manifestations. The South Devon project, reported by Burden in Chapter 5, appears to be particularly well thought out and it is therefore all the more disappointing that his team chose to assess the impact of their work through extremely 'soft' variables such as the 'degree of teacher commitment and feelings of empowerment'. It is unclear whether any use was made of objective indices of pupil behaviour in judging the overall effectiveness of the programme.

A cynic might therefore identify one advantage that family therapy does have over behavioural psychology. Though both are, properly understood, expressions of a humanistic ideology (that is with the belief that the purpose(s) of human life must be defined by people rather than being supplied ready made by God, the universe, fate, etc.), family therapy carries with it an aura of deep caring and cognitive complexity that the more overtly scientific behavioural approaches have largely avoided. Family therapy may have just that 'warm wetness' that positive teaching lacks.

Burden's apparent ignoring of data on pupil response is all the more curious given another aspect of his work. Following Wilson (1971), he draws an interesting distinction between control, which is manifested in orderly procedures, and discipline which involves a far more self-conscious rational evaluation of ends as well as means. The first is, of course, Weber's 'instrumental rationality', the latter his 'value rationality'. Presumably the order which accompanies discipline is logically entailed by the aims and values of the organisation rather than having a merely contingent relationship to them. Hence, discipline requires not just conformity but understanding. For Burden, the Elton Report and the DES (1987) Report entitled *Good Behaviour and Discipline in Schools* are mainly (and not wholly appropriately) concerned with order despite their recognition that the teaching of values is a major part of education. Thus, the Elton Report is censured for failing to define what is meant by good behaviour. One would expect then that the approach developed in South Devon would address 'discipline' as opposed to mere 'order', but if it does this is not clear to the reader. For example, the approach is described as having four characteristics but not one of them is concerned directly with the issue of the rationality of a school's goals. If 'socially oriented thinkers' were what was aimed for, then some orientation towards socially oriented thinking is called for.

Glynn also emphasises that school discipline is more than just control. The Elton Report has no doubt that pupil discipline relates to pupil self-control and maturity and that Personal and Social Education (PSE), as a subject which directly addresses the development of pupils as members of a community, is another potential victim of the Educational Reform Act (ERA). At the risk of generating a conspiracy view of affairs, one might remark that the current Conservative government may not be too upset by the threat to PSE. PSE, like explicitly argued discipline policies, carries the implication that all aspects of school discipline and pupil-teacher relationships should be open to rational discussion – the advance of rationalisation once again!

THE ELTON REPORT AND PROFESSIONALISM

The notion of professionalism in Britain is a vexed one. In terms of teaching it seems to come down to meaning immense accountability with decreasing authority. This is in contrast to the police who seem to be increasingly powerful and minimally accountable to the actual consumers. When teachers are claimed to be failing there is talk of shake ups and a need for greater productivity; when the police fail the talk is of employing more of them and paying them all more!

In Chapter 3 Ted Glynn addresses the issue of whole-school policies. He emphasises the need for a team approach and highlights some of the problems that this may bring. Teachers have traditionally valued their individual freedom of action. Whole-school discipline policies implicitly threaten this since consistency of approach demands prior agreement over what the discipline policy is actually to be in some detail. It may be that some teachers currently co-exist in the staffroom by tacitly agreeing to differ as to what is acceptable classroom behaviour.

This high degree of freedom from both outside interference in, and each other's scrutiny of, their classrooms may be another reason for the lack of hard data on classroom disruption. Once they have qualified teachers are typically left to get on with it unless utter mayhem breaks out. It may seem that to admit to discipline problems is to risk professional *harakiri* except where the pupil in question is publicly agreed to be a nuisance (in which case it becomes a personal problem for them, rather than a discipline problem for you!). Bennett emphasises the need for honesty and mutual support in the staffroom if this 'conspiracy of silence' is to be overcome.

Glynn also observes that good relationships with parents are called for by a whole-school approach. Here again he alerts us to potential value clashes. Teachers' representatives, like conservative ideologues, have focused upon increasing parental liability for their children's actions. However, the flip side of liability has to be some sort of authority for parents in the form of a say in school affairs, as the European Court of Justice's decision regarding corporal punishment has already demonstrated.

IMPLEMENTING CHANGE

Like Glynn, Burden (see Chapter 5) addresses the issue of whole-school behaviour policies. He has taken a major role in developing a partnership between a school psychological service team and a number of schools in the area that it serves. Burden's approach is avowedly eclectic; his ten-point plan is largely behavioural but includes counselling as well as exotica like reality therapy. Burden very sensibly emphasises the difficulties inherent in developing whole-school policies, in particular those concerned with achieving a 'critical mass' of involved staff, and the maintenance of directed change. His remarks echo those made regarding the difficulty of maintaining the effectiveness of behaviourally oriented teachers in schools where they are in a minority (see, for example, Merrett and Wheldall, 1984). Burden sees the role of outside consultants like educational psychologists, who can provide both a detached view and, also, continuing support, as particularly valuable here.

WHO ARE THE 'CONSUMERS' OF EDUCATION

There is, however, a further point concerning responsibility which Glynn does not raise. If we wish to talk of the consumers of education then it is clear that they are the pupils, not the parents, even though the latter pay for the education. The Elton Report does recognise this, calling for increasing pupil responsibility and involvement with age.

One does not have to have drunk deep of the writings of radical educationists to wonder whether in-school relationships should really be modelled upon a notion of hierarchy which is becoming extinct in adult society? Pupils' views of school discipline (in Wilson's sense), and what is appropriate in the classroom, are a little thin on the ground and yet they are important, not just in terms of achieving order, but also in relationship to the effects of various types of teaching style on actual learning. This is a point that the Elton Report touches upon and which is explored by Lewis and Lovegrove (1987). To its credit family therapy does take account of phenomenological aspects of classroom behaviour, that is the individual's account to him- or herself of what the meaning of their behaviour is. Likewise attribution theory, considered in another context by Hastings (1989), has taken pupils' interpretations of rewards and punishments seriously.

What of the wider, societal issues raised by the problem of school discipline? It is not wholly inappropriate to see school as a microcosm of society. What are children's motivations for participating in schooling? Putting it in its most extreme form one could claim that children are coerced into long hours of unpaid, unchosen and (possibly) unrewarding work. Society needs educated and trained individuals but what immediate pay-offs do they get from it? The press has recently carried reports of secondary schools giving (very infrequent) rewards for perfect attendance. Even these meagre remunerations are typically blazoned abroad as bribes. From a behavioural viewpoint, however, schools must, by definition, be rewarding – or nothing would ever get done. What are the rewards of schooling and how can we make them more powerful? Again, whilst we cannot tell whether or not schools are becoming more disorderly than they were, no such uncertainty surrounds the ever-growing crime rate. Should the real question be 'Why are children still relatively well behaved?' given the increasing criminality of their 'elders and betters'. Could it be that those crummy old teachers really do have an impact?

PROSPECTS FOR THE ELTON REPORT AND PSYCHOLOGY IN EDUCATION

Will the Elton Report lead to great things or will it be, as Bennett fears, stillborn? It looks rather as if it will be another, if unintended, victim of the National Curriculum. When schools should have been taking on board the Report's proposals they are, in fact, primarily engaged in coping with Local Management of Schools and preparing to implement the National Curriculum. All schools have received a copy of the Report but how many have managed to actually study it and act upon it?

Another victim? Herein lies the irony. Make no mistake; the National Curriculum calls for sacrifices – not just in school curricula but also in programmes of teacher training. More compulsory subjects mean more subject time and less time spent on those despised theories. And a major source of theories is – psychology. Hence, the possibility that whatever response psychologists outside of school psychological services make to Elton will be largely futile since no one will be giving them any room to intervene anyway. But take heart; if Dr Lawlor gets her way, this lack of psychology in teacher training will not matter. There will be no teacher training!

REFERENCES

Bernstein, B. (1970) 'Education cannot compensate for society', *New Society*, 387: 344–7.

Brubaker, R. (1984) *The Limits of Rationality: an essay on the social and moral theory of Max Weber*, London: Allen Lane.

DES (1987) *Education Observed 5, Good Behaviour and Discipline in Schools*, London: HMSO.

—— (1989) *Discipline in Schools (The Elton Report)*, London: HMSO.

Hastings, N. (1989) 'Making sense of the sense teachers make of effecting change in children's behaviour', *British Psychological Society Education Section Review* 14, 1: 31–6.

Jenks, C. (1975) *Inequality: a reassessment of the effect of family and schooling in America*, Harmondsworth: Penguin.

Lawlor, S. (1990) *Teachers Mistaught: training in theories or education in subjects*, London: Centre for Policy Studies.

Lewis, R. and Lovegrove, M.N. (1987) 'What students think of teachers' classroom control techniques: results from four studies', in N. Hastings and J. Schwieso (eds) *New Directions in Educational Psychology 2: behaviour and motivation in the classroom*, London: Falmer.

Merrett, F. and Wheldall, K. (1984) 'Training teachers to use the behavioural approach to classroom management: a review', *Educational Psychology* 4: 213–32.

—— (1987) 'Troublesome classroom behaviours', in N. Hastings and J. Schwieso (eds) *New Directions in Educational Psychology 2: behaviour and motivation in the classrooms*. London: Falmer.

Mortimore, P., Sammons, P., Stoll, L., Lewis, D. and Ecob, R. (1988) *School Matters: the junior years*, London: Open Books.

Pearson, G. (1983) *Hooligans: a history of respectable fears*, London: Macmillan.

Rutter, M., Maughan, B., Mortimore, P. and Ouston, J. (1979) *Fifteen Thousand Hours: secondary schools and their effects on pupils*, London: Open Books.
Wheldall, K. and Glynn, T. (1989) *Effective Classroom Learning: a behavioural interactionist approach to teaching*, Oxford: Basil Blackwell.
Wilson, P.S. (1971) *Interest and Discipline in Education*, London: Routledge & Kegan Paul.

Index

Note: page references have been given for the Elton Report only where it has been directly referred to by quotation.